THE NORTH CASCADES

Lyman Lake and Chiwawa Mountain in the Glacier Peak Wilderness

THE NORTH CASCADES

FINDING BEAUTY AND RENEWAL IN THE WILD NEARBY

BY WILLIAM DIETRICH

WITH CRAIG ROMANO, CHRISTIAN MARTIN, AND GARY SNYDER

FOREWORD BY RICHARD LOUV

BRAIDED RIVER

THE CONSERVATION IMPRINT OF MOUNTAINEERS BOOKS

CONTENTS

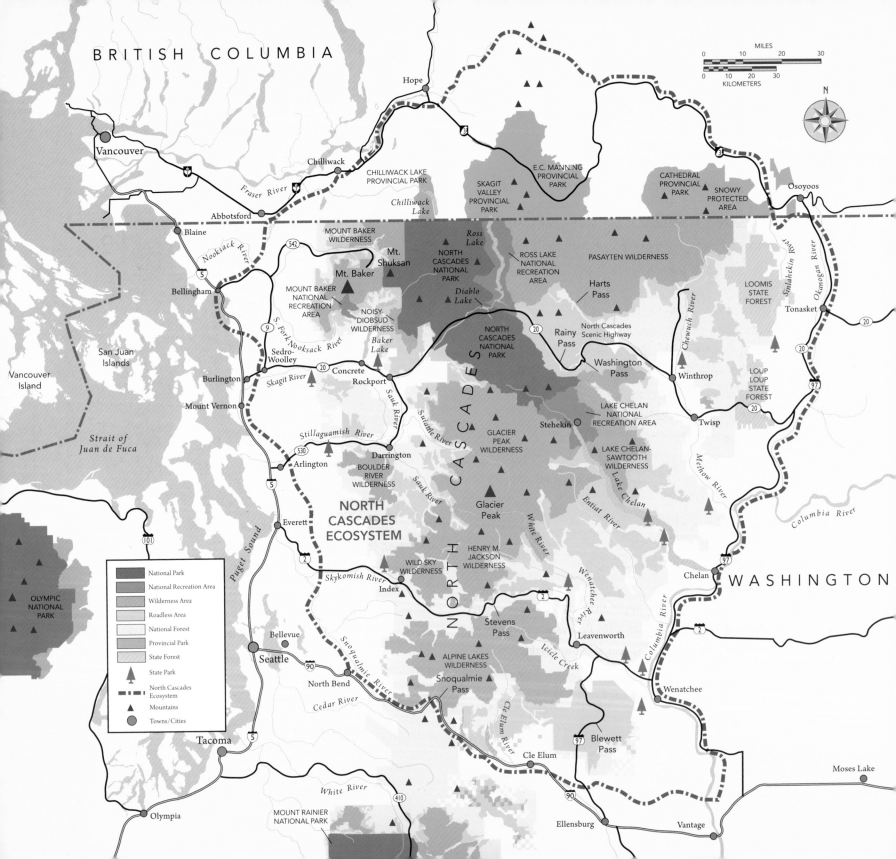

THE NORTH CASCADES ECOSYSTEM

The landscape of the North Cascades is bounded by the Fraser River on the north, the Okanogan Highlands and Columbia Plateau on the east, Snoqualmie Pass to the south, and the Puget lowlands to the west. Mountains, rising nearly from sea level, are the signature of this magnificent place. Fifteen peaks tower over 9,000 feet while nearly 300 rise in elevation between 7,000 and 9,000 feet.

The North Cascades Ecosystem comprises one of the most intact wildlands in the contiguous United States. The heart of this area lies under public management as North Cascades National Park; Ross Lake and Lake Chelan national recreation areas; Mount Baker-Snoqualmie and Okanogan-Wenatchee national forests; and the Glacier Peak, Pasayten, Mount Baker, Chelan-Sawtooth, Boulder River, Noisy-Diobsud, Alpine Lakes, Henry M. Jackson, Stephen Mather, and Wild Sky wilderness areas. North of the international border, much of the land is designated as Manning, Cathedral, and Chilliwack Lake provincial parks; the Skagit Recreation Area; the Snowy Protected Area; and in Provincial (Crown) Forests.

This spectacular region of coastal plain, rich lowland valleys, dense forests, spectacular mountain peaks, and arid shrub-steppe habitats encompasses approximately 28,000 square miles. Elevations in the North Cascades Ecosystem range from sea-level at Puget Sound to 10,781 feet at Mount Baker.

The largest watercourse in the North Cascades Ecosystem is the Columbia River, which gathers together all the waters of the

eastern slope and empties directly into the Pacific Ocean along the Washington–Oregon border.

Watersheds west of the crest drain directly into the inland marine waters of the Salish Sea, Puget Sound, and the Strait of Georgia. The largest of these west-slope rivers are the Skagit and the Fraser, the latter of which, with the Thompson River, is the only river to bisect the North Cascades, and thus serve as a low corridor connecting its dramatically different east and west sides.

—Thomas L. Fleischner and Saul Weisberg

See page 44, "The Lay of the Land," for more detail on the North Cascades ecosystem and page 178 for clarifications on Public Lands Designations.

Left: North Cascades Ecosystem Public Lands Designations (see pages 178–179 for more information on these designations.)

EARTH HOUSE HOLD

BY GARY SNYDER

SOURDOUGH MOUNTAIN LOOKOUT

19 July

Up at a quarter to six, wind still blowing the mist through the trees and over the snow. Rins'd my face in the waterhole at the edge of the snowfield—ringed with white rock and around that, heather. Put up the SX aerial on a long pole made by some lookout of years past, sticks & limbs & trunks all wired and tied together. Made a shelf for papers out of half an old orange crate, and turned the radio receiver off. Walked down the ridge, over the snow that follows so evenly the very crest—snow on the north slope, meadows and trees on the south. Small ponds, lying in meadows just off the big snowfields, snags, clumps of mountain hemlock, Alpine fir, a small amount of Alaska cedar.

Got back, built a fire and took the weather. About six, two bucks came, one three-point, one four-point, very warily, to nibble at huckleberries and oats and to eat the scraps of mouldy bacon I threw out. Shaggy and slender, right in the stiff wind blowing mist over the edge of the ridge, or out onto the snowfield, standing out clear and dark against the white. Clouds keep shifting—totally closed in; a moment later across to Pyramid Peak or up to Thunder Creek it's clear. But the wind stays.

Now I've eaten dinner and stuffed the stove with twisted pitchy Alpine fir limbs. Clumps of trees fading into a darker and darker gray. White quartz veins on the rocks out the south window look like a sprinkling of snow. Cones on the top boughs of the Alpine fir at the foot of the rocks a DARK PURPLE, stand perfectly erect, aromatic clusters of LINGAMS fleshy and hard.

Lookout free talk time on the radio band: Saul called Koma Kulshan, Church called Sauk, Higgins is talking to Miner's Ridge. Time to light the lamp.

Gary Snyder's artistry and wilderness ethic was honed during a fire-lookout summer in the North Cascades during the 1950s. He was born in San Francisco and raised on small farms in Washington and Oregon; his early experiences also included work as a seaman, logger, and trail crew member. He was awarded the Pulitzer Prize for his collection of poems Turtle Island. *This passage is an excerpt from his 1957 publication* Earth House Hold: Technical Notes and Queries to Fellow Dharma Revolutionaries.

Snowboarder descending the dock at Field's Point on Lake Chelan to board the Lady Express to Stehekin.

Students learn about the ecosystems, geology, and natural and cultural history of the mountains at North Cascades Institute's Mountain School. These environmental education programs are held in cooperation with North Cascades National Park and Seattle City Light.

FOREWORD
NATURAL KINSHIP

BY RICHARD LOUV

For anyone who has ever lived within visual range of the great mandibles of the Northwest, the North Cascades and the Olympics, the distant sawtooth ridges left their mark. My family lived for a year and a half in Seattle. From my attic office window, when the rain and mist lifted, I could see the Olympics. When my wife and I walked up the hill behind our house and looked toward the east, we could also see that other range of distant peaks, which somehow seemed more mysterious, a lost world. Exploring them, we saw and felt the massive strength of old-growth cedar and hemlock, saw the dark hanging moss, entered groves and open meadows pinned by shafts of light, emerged to the long sky and sudden granite spires sharp enough to pierce the heart. We were changed by the nature of this place, nurtured by its beauty, humbled by its danger. *The North Cascades: Finding Beauty and Renewal in the Wild Nearby* is a fitting title for the book you hold in your hands. Through photography and words, this book conveys the beauty of the landscape; its power to transform and renew human beings is more elusive, more easily felt than described. But you can sense it in these pages.

We hunger for authenticity. As the human-manufactured environment becomes more fabricated and virtual, the value of the natural world will grow in our eyes. Natural history will, or could be, as important to our personal and regional identities as human history, particularly in those places where human history has been interrupted or forgotten. In my book *The Nature Principle*, I describe the Northwest as a "purposeful place" because so many parts of it remain so brilliantly, even brutally authentic. It demands a sense of attachment; it has the power to shape dreams.

Over the past two decades, researchers have attempted to calibrate the benefits to human health of urban parks and wilderness forests, of rivers, of our contact with other species, of star-filled nights seen from a sleeping bag rolled out near a mountain meadow. A growing body of evidence indicates that people of every age who regularly recreate or learn in more natural environments are physically and mentally healthier, feel happier, and test better in school. Science can never take the full measure of the value of the natural world; in fact, scientists struggle to even define "nature" (we know it when we see it), in part because humans *are* nature—the watcher being watched. Nonetheless, a growing body of evidence, emphasizing the impact of nature experience on human health and cognitive abilities, does provide a fresh argument for the protection of wilderness and the expansion of nearby nature, but also for cities as potential engines of biodiversity. This argument includes but goes beyond the usual list of benefits such as clean air and drinking water, efficiently engineered watersheds, the extractive value of natural resources, and even traditional measures of beauty.

Ongoing studies by the Human-Environment Research Laboratory at the University of Illinois show that direct exposure to the outdoors—its flowers, trees, leaves, moss, fungi, and dirt; animals, large and small, winged and furred; and natural landscape and horizon—can significantly relieve symptoms of attention deficit hyperactivity disorder. Scientists at the University of Sheffield in the United Kingdom have found that the more species that live in a park, the greater the apparent psychological benefits to human beings. In related work, researchers at the University of Rochester, in New York, report that exposure to the natural environment appears to lead people to nurture close relationships with fellow human beings, to value community, and to be more generous with money. Kinship with the larger community of species, along with our affiliation with natural landscapes, can build our social capital and help us feel and be more alive.

This research, combined with common sense and millennia of human experience and our survival instinct, is encouraging the emergence of a new nature movement, one that reaches beyond the necessity of sustainability—a concept that much of the public now defines too broadly, as a vague goal, or too narrowly, as energy efficiency only. Yes, saving energy is fundamental, but more nature in our lives can also produce *human* energy—in the forms of better mental and physical health, sharper cognition,

more creativity and productivity, and the nourishment of spirit. As a result of this movement, nature-based schools are growing in number. The North Cascades Institute and other nature education organizations understand the potency of this movement and its power to renew individuals, families, and even businesses. Biophilic architects (who weave natural elements into every aspect of the human habitat), new agrarians who bring food production close to home, landscape architects and designers who renew yards and neighborhoods with native plants, ecopsychologists and nature therapists, and many others are widening the definition of green jobs. Some physicians, particularly pediatricians, now recommend nature time to their patients. In 2010, a pilot program in Portland, Oregon, began to pair physicians with park professionals, who will help fulfill "park prescriptions" and participate in a longitudinal study to measure the effect on health. Across the continent, families are banding together to create multiple-family nature clubs. We see a growing legion of citizen naturalists.

The three major environmental challenges of our time—climate change, the biodiversity collapse, and the disconnect between children and nature—are linked. Respect for the natural world and the ability to care deeply about pollution or vanishing species are usually born of firsthand knowledge. But even for those who never set foot among the hemlocks, knowledge of the North Cascades—perhaps first gained through the book in your hands—can enrich young lives and translate later into deeper attachment to this place and a greater constituency for its ongoing preservation. This book encourages us to go beyond the turning of pages, to personally, directly experience the silence of snowfields, the explosions of wildflowers, the shadows of rain and mist, and to carry those memories and pass them on.

My brief relationship with this region taught me how nature, if fully valued, can help build a sense of regional and personal identity. When my wife and son and I left Seattle and returned to San Diego, I came to see my own bioregion anew, as a purposeful place all its own. The North Cascades ecosystem, with its staggering beauty and wildness, can give that same gift to many others. This rugged chunk of the Northwest, so close to high-tech Seattle and Bellevue and all the growing cities of Puget Sound, is a regional, national, and worldwide resource of inestimable value, a reminder of who we are, a suggestion of who we could be.

The rushing waters of Downey Creek flow past blooming wildflowers, Glacier Peak Wilderness

The Pickets, a sub-range on the west side of Skagit Valley, draw out rain from maritime weather, creating a rainshadow on the east side that generates dry, sunny weather.

INTRODUCTION
THE WILD NEARBY

BY HELEN CHERULLO AND MARTINIQUE GRIGG

As our small plane dips, we gaze out the window and see climbers ascending prized summits. Their tiny shapes provide a sense of scale for this immense landscape of spires, spikes, mounds, valleys, and twisting river veins. The lowland trees and understory are intensely green. Directly below us is where a wolf pack is said to roam. Although we know it is futile, we can't help ourselves, and strain to catch a glimpse of the elusive creatures.

Clear water moves languidly in the wide rivers, then flashes with reflected light as it quickens into narrow streams. Glaciers fold and drape the sides of jagged mountains with telltale crystal-blue ice. And the towering peaks and crags of the North Cascades run on and on to the distant horizon.

We're flying with Matt Hyde. An avid outdoorsman, photographer, and pilot, he is an outdoor retailer by profession, with a stint at REI and now as CEO of West Marine. The North Cascades have provided him with years of adventure and wonder as a place of retreat, recreation, and renewal. He is showing us a god's-eye view of this wild refuge in the backyard of one of the most developed cities on the West Coast.

It is a landscape largely out of mind—off the beaten track, with limited access roads. To get out and back is physically and psychologically demanding. The land is rugged; you have to seek it.

This is a land defined and shaped by water. The 2.7 million acres of the North Cascades ecosystem are the source of clean water for over seven million people, as well as for farms and other life-sustaining industries. Quite a bit of what we see below us is public land, legislated and protected for citizens and visitors alike to freely enjoy as national park lands, wildernesses, and wild and scenic rivers (see pages 178–179 for more details on this). As the population of this special corner of the Pacific Northwest increases, there is no doubt that this land will be affected. Although much of it appears wild and protected, in reality, the North Cascades are in limbo.

In 1964, The Mountaineers published *The North Cascades*, a photographic book with images by Tom Miller, text by Harvey Manning, and maps by Dee Molenaar. In 1968, North Cascades National Park was established by an act of Congress, and that book was credited with contributing to its passage. In 1971, The Mountaineers published *The Alpine Lakes*, written by Brock Evans and edited by Manning, with images by Ed Cooper and Bob Gunning, to celebrate the southern part of the North

Cascades, and it was similarly influential. President Gerald Ford had decided to veto the Alpine Lakes Wilderness legislation, but changed his mind after Washington State's governor, Dan Evans, gave him a copy of the book. Its stunning photographs of these glorious mountains and forests transported the president back to precious boyhood memories. Ford signed the act in 1976.

When we recently talked with Evans about our plans to publish a new book on the North Cascades, he said, "I wish there was such a book that I could pass around. It worked like a charm last time."

So, in 2010, we convened more than twenty leaders of conservation organizations at The Mountaineers Program Center in Seattle. We shared our concerns for the health of this nearby ecosystem—so close that its peaks can be seen from the city. We said we knew there would be threats related to development: housing, roads, timber, mining, recreation, tourism, water use, pollution, climate change. Could we work together and get ahead of the wave of rapid change and development?

We asked this group if it was time to publish a *new* book that describes the North Cascades ecosystem and the wide variety of life it sustains. We acknowledged that many in the room held differing opinions on what should be preserved and how—and that our intent was not to take sides, but to provide a story of *why* the natural value of this place should be preserved, while the organizations settle on the *how*. It will take time to define and build a public ethic of protection. As this unfolds, solutions will surface, and be argued and debated—ultimately resulting in necessary legislation that will provide lasting protection for these critical lands and waters. In the meantime, we could take this story to the people, to the press, and to our elected officials.

Although many in the room did not agree on a course of legislative action, we were surprised that—to a person—*everyone* agreed that a book of this kind would be a critical tool in upcoming preservation campaigns.

So we got to work. William Dietrich wrote of the abundant life, intriguing geology, and complex human history of the region in an essay that takes readers on a tour through the North Cascades. Gary Snyder honored us by contributing poems from his North Cascades journals—with personal insights that pierce the imagination. A variety of people who characterize the land came to life through Christian Martin's perceptive interviews; and ways to experience the area on foot, by boat, and by car were carefully selected by Craig Romano to show the variety of life, landscape, recreation, and scenic wonders within the greater ecosystem. And the North Cascades Institute, under Saul Weisberg's leadership, became our partner in taking this volume beyond the bookstore—and into classrooms and communities.

The images and stories in this book speak to our memories, to our hearts, and to something deep within us that values the idea of preserving beauty for future generations. You are holding our hopes for the future of the North Cascades—*the wild nearby*—in your hands.

Helen Cherullo
Publisher
Mountaineers Books

Martinique Grigg
Executive Director
The Mountaineers

A climber high on the west ridge of Mount Stuart, a peak protected within the Alpine Lakes Wilderness Area

Salmon—including these coho—are born in freshwater, feed and mature at sea, and return to the streams of their birth to spawn a new generation. Only one out of a thousand salmon may survive the journey.

A hiker strolls next to a reflecting pond near Park Butte on the south side of Mount Baker. Elevations in the North Cascades range from sea level at the Salish Sea to 10,781 feet at Mount Baker. These vastly different places are separated by only thirty miles.

THE NORTH CASCADES
WILD BY DESIGN

BY WILLIAM DIETRICH

I was introduced to the power of the North Cascades by a midnight 1972 trek up Coleman Glacier. Newly married, my wife, Holly, and I had joined a mountain climbing class offered through Fairhaven College in nearby Bellingham, and 10,781-foot Mount Baker was our culminating ascent. While a modest climb by global standards, Baker's fifteen square miles of ice loom well above civilization's envelope, and striding up a glacier—named for Edmund Coleman, who in 1868 was the first to summit the peak—was exotic. We were Northwest natives, familiar with the region's mountains, but the North Cascades Highway was still four months from officially opening and the pinnacles crammed against Canada had an over-the-horizon mystery. They were, and are, Washington's highest mountains on average, as well as its steepest, grandest, and most remote. North Cascades National Park was less

than four years old and was the nation's wildest park outside of Alaska.

The range was still locked in snow that wet spring—winter dominates from October to May—and each weekend climb had been hampered by weather. Dangerous cornices had turned back my portion of the class when we had tried to reach the summit of one of the Twin Sisters. (Holly's section was successful on the northern peak.) During another outing, half the students had been buried waist-deep in a small avalanche. We'd camped in snow, slogged in snow, and sweated in snow.

With cold came beauty, the frosted peaks melodramatic and alluring. Each outing was a step through the looking glass.

The glaciated volcano is fifteen miles south of the international border. To summit, we hiked the commonest route to Kulshan Cabin, first built in 1925 by the Mount Baker Club

Mount Baker and Coleman Glacier

and gone now. We fitfully rested in its 1951 replacement before being roused at midnight to climb before the sun turned the snow mushy. The clear night sky was the best weather we'd had. Our flashlights were hardly needed, the glacier glowing pearl under the moon. Bellingham's lights formed a distant galaxy below. Ahead was challenge and clarity. Cascades volcanoes dwarf, with Antarctic grandeur, those who climb them.

Baker was named for a British third lieutenant who spotted it on Captain George Vancouver's expedition of 1792. The Indian name was Koma Kulshan, or at least that was a pioneer amalgam of words from the Lummi and Nooksack tribes. The usual translation is "Great White Watcher," but in his 1984 history, *Koma Kulshan*, author John Miles finds otherwise. He cites sources that define *kulshan* either as a Lummi word meaning "damaged peak," since Baker was a volcano, or as derived from the Nooksack phrase *kwómae kwelsáen*, meaning "go up high or way back in the mountains shooting," or hunting. Early settlers struggled to pronounce and understand Salish languages, and the Nooksack name for Baker, *kwéq smáenit* (White Mountain), is difficult to make lyrical in English.

To me it was simply exotic. We climbed in rope teams for safety, but the crevasses were still bridged with snow. The glacier's surface was crusty and our progress was a strenuous but steady slog. Stars faded, the sky went from black to cobalt blue, and then the summit glowed orange, as imposing as a pyramid.

When we reached a saddle at nine thousand feet, between Colfax Peak and the main volcanic cone, my weary wife and another woman decided to wait while the rest of us summited. The steep climb up the forty-degree Roman Wall was not technical, but it required the kicking of snow steps, ice axes ready for arrest. I recall a lot of panting.

Dawn lit the world. Light danced on cornices of snow that leaned out from the Black Buttes, turning them butter. My bride was a tiny dot in a spotless amphitheater more than a thousand feet below. Then, as feeble heat focused and I watched with alarm, avalanches began to peel and thunder toward the women, implacable as gravity.

There was nothing to do but watch. Snow cracked, hissed, plunged, hit, and shot across the saddle, the prow tumbling like the blades of a reel mower. The pair hurriedly retreated from a slide that came within ten yards. More avalanches came down, spilling farther. They backed up some more. The dance seemed choreographed. A crack, a roar, and human flight up the other slope of the saddle. Finally the dawn cannonade ceased and it was quiet again. The women warily sat. This was before cellphones or inexpensive radios, and only the mountain was doing the talking. We'd been taught the danger: Baker has had at least 18 climbing deaths; Mount Rainier, 114.

We summited. To the east was a wilderness of peaks painted Williamsburg blue, rising from pockets of cloud. The vista was cold, exhilarating, and breathless. We took our pictures and then used our axes as brakes to glissade back down to the broken fingers of the avalanches. What had looked like sifted flour from above were snow boulders as big as cars when I reached Holly.

That adventure became the summit of our mountain climbing career; we've left gravity to others. I've never lost my respect for the North Cascades.

I've never lost my sense of wonder, either. The volcano was ethereal from the blues and chocolate of its ice and rock, and when I've hiked its flanks since, the beauty and scale never fail to dazzle. Challenge hones the experience of these peaks. There are higher mountains in the world but few that feel so pristine, so uncompromising, so steep, and so wet. "They get heavy snow that sticks like whipped cream," says Saul Weisberg, a former ranger who now directs the educational North Cascades Institute.

The North Cascades are so near and yet so far, so simple to appreciate and yet so difficult to manage and understand, so seductive and so stormy. I've hiked, camped, skied, rafted, canoed, learned, taught, and (with the wisdom of age) sampled wines in the vineyards of their eastern foothills. I'd need several more lifetimes to fully know the range.

In the more than four decades since my climb, Bellingham has doubled in size. So have the metropolitan populations of Seattle, Vancouver, British Columbia, and all the smaller communities in between, on both sides of the range. Subdivisions have spread like moss. Freeways have swollen, resorts plopped down, and organic farmers sprouted amid cow pastures and stump farms. We've added GPS, SUVs, Gore-Tex, iPads, major league sports, opera, grunge, artisanal cooking, and trailhead parking permits.

The mountains abide.

The North Cascades are surrounded by seven million people, crisscrossed by jetliners, and threaded by highways. Their retreating glaciers have become a barometer of climate change. At the same time, grizzly, wolf, wolverine, and eagle, once shot and trapped, are coming back. There is a new Environmental Learning Center across Diablo Dam, and new philosophies about forest fires, ecosystem management, and outdoor recreation. The North Cascades are exactly the same, and completely different.

Life in the Pacific Northwest has accelerated. Microsoft and Amazon have supplanted resource-based companies such as Weyerhaeuser as economic drivers. Computers have globalized us. We've all become minutemen, with once-a-day mail delivery giving way to minute-by-minute email, Facebook posts, and Twitter feeds. An entire vocabulary of technical jargon has been mastered, society has become more diverse, and newcomers have injected their own take, deciding to call Puget Sound "the" Puget Sound, out of our inexplicable drive to complicate everything. Manual labor has given way to sedentary jobs, and in response camping and backpacking equipment has gone high-tech and recreational choices have exploded. We're connected, busy, isolated, worldly, and stressed. Accordingly, the North Cascades represent escape and self-fulfillment. They beckon as last-stand glory, temple, and playground.

There is the reality of the mountains, that difficult terrain wracked by evolving change. "It is incredibly wild," says Chip Jenkins, a former North Cascades National Park superintendent now serving as deputy regional director. "It is raw. It is physically and psychologically demanding." And there is the ideal of the mountains, a place frozen into a calendar photo. The North Cascades are besieged and yet sacrosanct. They are eternal, and yet their purpose is constantly being reinvented in our minds.

Tucked into the fourth corner of the United States, these mountains were the last to be explored. They are still remote, jungle-dense on their western slopes, and relatively unknown. Fjord-narrow lakes wind into the mountain fastness; it is a fifty-five-mile boat trip from Chelan to the mountain hamlet of Stehekin in Lake Chelan National Recreation Area, at the southeastern edge of North Cascades National Park. The North Cascades Highway, opened in 1972, brings three-quarters of a million people through a corridor between the two halves of that park each summer season, but only twenty-six thousand walk

A climber ascends a rocky step on a high ridge winter traverse in the South Picket Range in North Cascades National Park.

Lenticular clouds glow in the sunset in the Picket Range in North Cascades National Park.

far enough from their cars to enter the park proper. Gettysburg Battlefield gets more visitors in a busy weekend than the half-million-acre park gets in a year. It is deliberately roadless. You have to seek it.

The park is also truncated. Because of political compromise, Mount Baker is outside the national park "complex" (which technically includes the park lands and adjacent national recreation areas). So is the other glaciated volcano in the range, Glacier Peak. There is a bewildering patchwork of land designations, a contentiously debated road network, and a consortium of agencies.

Which brings us to peril. Visionaries protected this range over many decades of political battle in the twentieth century.

What one sees today from the summit of Mount Baker—craggy Mount Shuksan, the fanged Picket Range, the ice cream mound of Glacier—now needs a new generation of stewardship. How shall we manage these crags? Can their complex succession of ecosystems be sustained? Will salmon survive in the rivers? Will grizzlies, wolves, and wolverines roam? How can the North Cascades be resilient in the face of climate change? Since 1915, average air temperatures at Diablo Dam on the Skagit River have risen about 1 degree Fahrenheit, global warming shrinking the average snowpack. Can an alpine environment thrive if adjacent lowlands are paved over? Can we help native plants and organisms resist invasive species? How can a growing and aging urban

A hoary marmot in Boston Basin, North Cascades National Park. Hoary marmots live at high elevations above timberline in sub-alpine and alpine zones, occupying regions where there are few human inhabitants. They hibernate for over eight months a year, beginning in mid-September. Colonies snuggle together to conserve heat.

population visit this landscape without overpowering it? What does wilderness mean when it abuts a megalopolis of thickening development that stretches from Vancouver, British Columbia, to Eugene, Oregon?

In a frenzied world, the North Cascades are a refuge of calm. In a warming world, they are a remnant of the Ice Age. In a homogenous world, they remain exotic. In a crowded world, they are empty.

They are best befriended on foot.

FROM RIVER VALLEY TO RIDGE TOP

An imaginary hike in this region, on a fictional trail, a representative composite, would begin at the base of the steepest, most glaciated mountains in the conterminous United States, in a forest canyon so deep that it becomes dappled with light only after the sun has arced high into the summer sky. These are not America's highest mountains, mostly topping out at eight to nine thousand feet. But they start from valleys a mile or more below and reach toward heaven in an awful hurry. The "American Alps" are as precipitous as if a child drew them, carved by waterfall, draped by ice, garlanded by wildflowers, and decorated by a thousand alpine lakes. Glaciated Mount Shuksan, a buttress of the range's western flank, is frequently declared "the most photographed mountain in the world." Paparazzi-like ranks of shutterbugs line Picture Lake as if a movie star is happening by. The North Cascades include the nation's deepest chasm, flooded by glacial Lake Chelan, its heaviest snowfalls, and one of its most scenic highways.

The region spans international boundaries. In Washington it includes one national park, three national recreation areas, three national forests, nine wilderness areas, and the Loomis State Forest. In British Columbia's portion, there are three provincial parks, one protected area, and one recreation area. This region is the largest contiguous body of protected lands along the four-thousand-mile US–Canadian border, totaling 2.7 million acres. That is half a million acres bigger than Yellowstone National Park, or thirty times the size of the city of Seattle.

Fire lookout atop Desolation Peak, where the writer and Beat poet Jack Kerouac spent the summer of 1956 as a US Forest Service fire lookout in what was then the Mount Baker National Forest. Hozomeen Mountain is to the right.

The rambunctious tangle of mountains exhausted explorers, defeated miners, and captured the souls of novelists and poets. They are a place to contemplate existence and, in the phrase of Forest Service lookout and famed author Jack Kerouac, "the void." The writer of *On the Road* mused about the terror of existence when he was a fire lookout on Desolation Peak in 1956, high enough to look down on "marshmallow cloud." Lace up your boots. "The closer you get to real matter, rock air fire and wood, boy, the more spiritual the world is," Kerouac wrote in *The Dharma Bums*.

On our fictional trail in early morning, we walk along a creek that cuts a ribbon through the thickly forested alpine valley, the water white where it tumbles and bottle green where it drifts. The sky, past trees two hundred feet high, is narrow as a skylight. The water runs over shelves of rock veined with quartz, bubbling like champagne. In pools, the rocks are bright as copper pennies. This is water lifted from the nearby Pacific Ocean, deposited in torrents of rain or snow and tumbled back to salt chuck with hardly time to gets its toes dirty. Unless it comes off the snout of a glacier, the water is so transparent that at times it seems almost not there. And yet water is the essential, binding element of these mountains. Ice crowns them, rain sculpts them, and moisture cloaks them with forest.

Every late summer and fall, Pacific salmon return. Turned black, red, and hook-snouted, they muscle upstream, spew eggs and sperm over gravel nests, and die. Bears flip and browse, and fish carcasses feed hundreds of bald eagles wintering from Montana, Alaska, and Canada. The salmon runs represent ecological unity, tying the highest peak to estuarine marsh and ocean. The fish bring energy accumulated from the sea to the North Cascades foothills, their rot nourishing the forest.

On a summer day the shallows are seemingly empty (an illusion) and the damp cliff on the opposite shore is shaggy with moss. It sheds in places like the fur of the mountain goats that pick their way on pinnacles like ballerinas. The goats easily stay well out of reach. Radio-tagged animals have traveled from Harts Pass, on the eastern side of the range near Mazama, to Hozomeen Mountain at the Canadian border, a crow-flies distance of about forty miles, in a day and a half.

Down in the valley bottom, plant life explodes. Every crevice on the cliff face is an improbable home to fern, twisting vine maple, and tenacious Douglas fir bending toward the sky. As the light grows, the atmosphere seems tinted green. These mountain valleys get up to 160 inches of precipitation a year. The snow line constantly moves up and down in winter, but the average has climbed six hundred feet in the last fifty years, calculates Jon Riedel, geologist at North Cascades National Park. Despite that trend, the ski area of Mount Baker holds the world record for recorded snowfall in a single season: ninety-five feet in 1998–99, or nearly as high as three Olympic diving platforms stacked atop each other.

Travel just eighty miles east to the mountains' boundary at the Okanogan River, and annual precipitation dips as low as ten inches. The kingdom of moss gives way to the empire of grass and sagebrush. The western doorstep to the North Cascades is the island-dotted and rainy Puget Sound lowland. The eastern back porch is the channeled scablands of the Columbia Plateau.

Between these extremes, the North Cascades are not just mountains, but an orchestra of air, wind, water, ice, lightning, fire, avalanche, and a resulting diversity of life, from bugling elk in the valleys to ice worms on glaciers. The worms are not a myth. The quarter-inch-long creatures surface at evening to feed

An eastern cottontail forages in the grass near Cheam Lake Wetlands Regional Park in Chilliwack, British Columbia.

Fresh snow on Mount Pearce and the Chilliwack River

on algae and pollen before sinking at dawn into the safety of the ice. The North Cascades Glacier Climate Project estimated seven billion worms on Glacier Peak's Suiattle Glacier alone.

There are deer, beaver, otter, prowling cougar, and returning wolf, wolverine, and grizzly. Far from being a static postcard, the North Cascades are a place of eruption, erosion, evolution, and recovery. The peaks are so striking because they're so restless. North America will override about eighteen feet of the Juan de Fuca oceanic plate offshore and lift these peaks an average of three inches higher in an eighty-year period. Erosion will whittle the crags down by about the same amount. This is scenery as grand opera, its fluted ridges crystalized music.

The fangs and horns have inspired names worthy of Middle Earth. Above are mountains named Torment, Forbidden, Terror, Stiletto, Needle, Snagtooth, Bulls Tooth, Paul Bunyans Stump, Golden Horn, Challenger, and Triumph. There are Damnation Peak, Devils Park, Nightmare Camp, Last Chance Pass, Big Devil, Little Devil, Devils Thumb, Devils Stairway, Devils Dome, Devils Smokestack, and Devils Peak. There are Majestic Mountain, Eldorado, Storm King, Thunder, Stormy, Gunsight, and Highchair.

There is whimsy as well. Sourdough Peak is where prospector Jack Rowley in 1877 slipped and spilled a pail of sourdough starter. Kodak Peak in the Alpine Lakes Wilderness is where a Forest Service ranger lost a camera. There is Bears Breast (a sanitized government renaming of Bare Breast?), Leprechaun Lake, Chocolate Glacier, Poodle Dog Pass, Mix-Up Peak, and Whistling Pig Creek. ("Whistle-pig" is a pioneer name for the hoary marmot that inhabits the rocky meadows.) North Cascades National Park Complex alone has ninety mountains

higher than seven thousand feet. Rangers, surveyors, prospectors, and explorers went giddy in their naming.

The grandeur has drawn Hollywood for eighty years, with the North Cascades serving as backdrop for such big- and small-screen offerings as *Call of the Wild, Lassie Come Home, The Deer Hunter, Lost Horizon* (1973 version), *The Parallax View, Harry and the Hendersons, High Ice, This Boy's Life,* and *Twin Peaks.* It was when *Call of the Wild* was filmed at Baker's Heather Meadows in the winter of 1934–35 that the road to that mountain shoulder was first kept open year-round. In 1937 the first rope tow went in. Today there are two day lodges and eight ski lifts.

Nature's construction method can be seen in the shady valley bottoms. We hear pretty creek song, and waterfalls draw chalk lines on the cliffs above as fine as thread. But the spring deluge clears swaths of forest, heaps up tangles of gray snags, and lays down new gravel bars that are an archeology of mountain history. Rocks have tumbled as a result of earthquake, avalanche, flood, and volcano. Ice age glaciers deposited boulders.

The seemingly sterile creeks are a complex biotic soup. Insects rain in from the foliage, rocks are slippery with algae, and underneath are empires of aquatic bugs and larvae to feed the fat trout that hang like blimps above. Even flipping rocks does not reveal the extent of stream ecosystems. In the biggest valleys, the aquatic zone can be as much as thirty feet deeper and a mile wider than the visible river, all of it filled with life.

The cascades of the Cascades bring nutrients down. Salmon swim them back up. Everything is a cycle: the rock rising and eroding, the sea contributing precipitation that rushes back to saltwater, plants erupting and then dying back under the snow to nourish their successors, goats and bears moving high to feed and then drifting back down through autumn mists, falcons and hawks gliding with them. The North Cascades are wheels of time within wheels of time.

Dominating the mountain valleys near the creeks are deciduous trees such as pioneering alder, fast-growing big-leaf maple, and fat and spongy cottonwood, its fluffy seeds filling the air. Pink fireweed loves any scar left by fire or flood, and salmonberry and thimbleberry spread broad leaves to the wedge of sunlight. Hazel, dogwood, elderberry, Indian plum, Sitka ash, and gooseberry engulf logs like a Mayan jungle.

On our virtual hike, we start up. Our creek has cut a ravine through valley floors paved fifteen thousand years ago with ice age gravel. When we climb from creekside to a flat rocky bench, the forest changes to western red cedar, the most venerated

and valuable tree to Native Americans of the Northwest. Cedar thrives where roots stay wet, and like other North Cascades conifers it can exceed two hundred feet in height and a dozen feet in diameter. In the heart of the North Cascades, along Big Beaver Creek, the oldest trees are a thousand years old and fifteen feet wide.

Historically cedar was a partner. Its soft wood could be split into planks for longhouses, hollowed for canoes, or bent and carved into boxes. Its bark grows in strips like loose tape. Indian women cut a third of the way around the trunk and peeled upward until the bark broke at the top, leaving a scar like a triangular sail. The strips were made into rope, twine, cloaks, and skirts. The softest inner bark made diapers. The cedar was a spirit tree, and the trees held magic. The federal government has put cedars of cultural importance off-limits to logging and development.

Bunchberry carpets the forest floor in Mount Baker–Snoqualmie National Forest.

On our trail, the soft duff gives way to mineral soil. We traverse the classic Cascades lowland forest of Douglas fir and western hemlock, trunks sturdy as industrial smokestacks. The average biomass of a western Washington old-growth forest at this elevation—its weight of wood, needles, and leaves—is roughly twice that of tropical jungle. Trees fill every possible space. A fir straddles the mossy boulder from which it sprouted, its buttress roots squeezing the rock like fat thighs. A file of cedar growing from a nurse log supports a half-fallen western hemlock like Marines raising a flag. Another tree has tilted sideways, broken, and sprouted vertically again as high as a mast.

Slanting sunbeams are green-gold, dust motes like pixie dust, but dryness is an anomaly. The norm is overcast sponge.

Roughskin newt on artist's fungus in a rainforest of North Cascades National Park

Plants are a magic trick of sunlight, water, and air and encase water like balloons. The trees of this wet forest hold 250,000 gallons of water per acre. The trees in turn support worlds of life. Some branches are so insulated with moss that they look like arms in woolly sleeves. Epiphytes, or plants that grow on plants, root on the limbs, a hundred feet in the air, their roots feeding from, and feeding, the tree. Bark is camouflaged with lichens growing so thick in the rain that their volume can equal a fifth of a host tree's foliage.

The microscopic is where the action is. The recycling work of bacteria and insects is mostly invisible to us, but the seemingly quiet woods are factories of decay and recycling. Underground networks of tiny fungal threads can total miles per cubic inch of soil. A single fungus can cover acres—these organisms represent some of the largest on the planet, marking their presence by shoving up mushrooms. Fallen logs swell, rot, and burst, hatching a riot of insects and amphibians. The rot and regrowth emphasize the brevity of our lives and mock the importance we put on birth and death. Were your corpse to sink into this mossy carpet, its atoms would be reincarnated as a tree.

We're still learning the interdependence of forest species. Pileated woodpeckers peck out nesting cavities in dead trees and feed on carpenter ants. The ants in turn manage herds of aphids, milking them for a sugary secretion while breaking down wood. Other birds, bats, and flying squirrels use the woodpecker holes.

The sheer athletic ability of animals is astounding. Black swifts fly ten to twelve hours and hundreds of miles a day catching insects. Loons dive six hundred feet in pursuit of fish. A cougar can sprint twice as fast as an Olympic athlete, jump to a second-story balcony, and bite with a ton of force per square inch. Bald eagle eyesight is so superb that the birds can spot fish

Downed trees and snags in various states of decay form the rich biological foundation of an old-growth forest.

in the water from hundreds of feet above and are recorded as recognizing another eagle at distances of forty miles. Deer can clear eight-foot barriers and broad jump thirty feet.

The heart of a shrew can beat 1,200 times a minute when active, while the heart of a hoary marmot can slow to five beats when hibernating. A bear can sleep half the year without drinking or urinating.

Salal, sword fern, devil's club, and Oregon grape form an understory so dense that a detour off the trail can get you terribly lost. Indians, prospectors, hunters, trappers, and climbers bushwhacked anyway, displaying a hardiness matched by only the best athletes today. In the 1912 Mount Baker Marathon, a logger named Harvey Haggard rode forty-four miles from Bellingham to Glacier by train, ran fourteen miles to the

volcano's summit, fourteen miles back down, and returned by train in a total of nine hours and fifty-one minutes. Another finisher rode his bike twenty miles to start the race and twenty miles back home.

Look up. The first branches begin a hundred feet overhead, leading to the canopy world of owls, flying squirrels, red tree voles, and seabirds called marbled murrelets that nest as much as fifty miles from the ocean.

Look down. There are 3,400 species of insect and spider so far identified on or under the soil in the North Cascades, most invisibly small. You can unwittingly be standing on 120,000 insect legs with every boot step. Interacting with the bugs are worms, bacteria, and fungi that feed from, and feed, the roots of plants clawing for the sun. Calypso orchids rely on the insects

The subtle colors of a grasshopper blend with a pasque flower.

and fungi for germination and growth. A teaspoon of moist soil can contain more microorganisms than there are humans on Earth. Bacterial ecosystems have been traced a mile deep, and some scientists postulate that there is more biomass under the earth than atop it.

These mountains are a ladder of microclimates made by elevation, rainfall, and soil type. The North Cascades have America's greatest variety of wildflowers and vascular plants outside the Great Smoky Mountains, and as we hike through them we spy trillium, fairybells, currant, Nootka rose, snowberry, and ocean spray. We dine on salmonberry, thimbleberry, and huckleberry. Be careful what you touch, however, because some organisms defend themselves with nettles. Others discourage grazing with poisons. The botanical beauty with leaves as big as dinner plates and red-spike flowers is devil's club, a colonizer that chokes rocky ravines with toxic spines and mildly poisonous berries. Bushwhackers curse it, but tribes used the thin bark as an herbal cure-all and its thorny stems to snag fish.

Our trail switchbacks up the steep slope of geology's "angle of repose" at which the mountain has temporarily stabilized. Looking horizontally into the forest canopy, we get a squirrel's-eye view. We are in wilderness old growth, never logged, and thus variable in structure and species. Limbs are torn and twisted by wind. Shade-loving hemlock grows in the shadow of sun-loving Douglas fir, waiting its turn at forest succession. Fir bark as thick as battleship armor is blackened by periodic fire. Sap runs out in sheets like candle wax to ward off insect invaders. Fungal conks make steps for gnomes and elves.

In the early years of American forestry, the ragged look of mature forests was believed decadent. Logs rotted on the ground. Dead snags stood gray and ghostly. Monster trees decayed from the inside out, disintegrating when they finally keeled over. Why not replace this waste, early foresters reasoned, with a fresh new forest of young trees? They annihilated almost all old growth at lower elevations.

Further research revealed that nature knew best. Downed logs teem with insects and amphibians. Those pockmarked snags were apartment houses for birds that keep beetle infestations in check. The clearings punched by wind and fire opened the forest to diversity. Toppled trees became nurseries and left gaps in which owls could fly and hunt.

The human forest fuzzing the foothills is a monoculture of pygmies, harvested at between forty and eighty years old. Our natural forest is a complex ecology of growth balancing rot, trees adding to their girth even as they decay inside. It is chaos in ruthless balance, untidy and scarred. One study counted five major fires on Desolation Peak since 1851, with smaller ones occurring on average every fifteen years. Each blaze doomed some organisms and made room for others.

Rising further, our trail now steepens in earnest. If you haven't cursed the North Cascades—if your thighs haven't burned and your shoulders protested and your lungs gasped, if you haven't peered upward in vain for an end to the enclosing forest, if you haven't gaped in disbelief at miserly mileage markers, if you haven't sweated, ached, groaned and gulped, if you haven't rued the very day you were born . . . well, you simply haven't hiked enough switchbacks. Sourdough Mountain, Desolation Peak, Monogram Lake, Crater Mountain, Three Fool's Trail—these build character like a Puritan preacher.

Mosquitoes, flies, and wasps sometimes add torment; a 1933 photo of a highway survey crew at Washington Pass shows men swathed against bugs like a cross between Bedouins and beekeepers. District engineer Richard Carroll remembers other hazards: "There were many occasions when a pack train would encounter a bear and this would lead to one of the finest rodeos you have ever seen. Bucking horses over the mountain side, mules scattering packs, and then several hours to several days of gathering." On the drier eastern slopes, men shot plenty of rattlesnakes, too.

Even the early railroad trains had to switchback up Stevens Pass, five switchbacks on the west side and three on the east to make the 4,056-foot summit. At Horseshoe Tunnel, the engineer emerging from one end could look across the canyon at the train's caboose entering the other. To get rid of switchbacks, a 2.5-mile tunnel was completed by 1900. Then, when avalanches from logged slopes killed ninety-six passengers and crew in a 1910 disaster, and fifty to sixty more workers died in 1913, excavation began on today's eight-mile railroad tunnel under the pass. Opened January 12, 1929, it remains the longest railroad tunnel in the United States.

Switchbacks make you question your very sanity, but they allow you to forget normal irritation. Toiling upward, back and forth, brings the kind of exhaustion to mend broken hearts, obliterate tyrannical bosses, render stock market gyrations trivial, and forgive your own cocktail party embarrassments. What reward comes from such self-flagellation! Surely, surely, the top must be near! No, only another switchback. And another. And another.

A moment of philosophy is in order. The American instinct is to attack these peaks, to set a goal and pick a destination, to get where we are going and to get there fast. This mania is a legacy of pioneering history, drilled into us from the earliest days of our goal-oriented, grade-advancing, exam-centric schools.

Switchbacks exist to be conquered, mountains to be summited, and lakes to be circumnavigated.

Consider another worldview. Tap your inner Buddhist monk or Native American sensibility. Is it the destination, or the journey? Do you want triumph, or enlightenment?

A naturalist could discover the universe in a bend in the trail. A fold holds a trickle, the mountainside leaking after weeks of no rain, and a flower garden takes a drink. An avalanche erases a swath of forest and is recolonized by Sitka alder, jutting from the slide like the abatis of a fort. A log crumbles into punk when you touch it, and a salamander scurries away. Water chimes. Insects buzz. Trees sigh and creak, murmuring a secret language. Delicately veined leaves seem painted. Cones spiral in mathematical pattern. Horsetails date back to the dinosaurs.

When national park archeologist Bob Mierendorf first went looking for evidence of Indian habitation of the North Cascades, he spent two months observing: "It was only when I took the time to understand what was normal that I began to see what was abnormal. All of a sudden I started finding archeological sites all over the place. When you slow down and are patient, discoveries come to you." He stumbled on the aboriginal chert quarries near Hozomeen Mountain by hearing the grind of prehistoric flint-knapping flakes under his boots. The evidence was lying there. Someone had to listen to it.

What the North Cascades demand—their only ticket for entry, really—is that you pay attention. "That's the way you learn," poet and fire lookout Gary Snyder told author John Suiter for his book, *Poets on the Peaks*. "Sitting still and being quiet in nature. Then things start happening around you."

Go half as fast to see twice as much. Make every switchback a bead in a contemplative rosary. Make every pause a prayer.

Vibrant green old-man's-beard drapes over trees in an old-growth forest in the Alpine Lakes Wilderness. This lichen is one of many species found in the North Cascades.

Chert-flaking debris. Hozomeen chert is a distinctive, fine-textured rock that indigenous people used to create tools. The oldest known quarry in the region is estimated at 8,400 years of age.

Listen to the crack as glaciers calve and avalanche. Notice how many spider webs hang in the shrubs. Count the animal burrows at the base of trees. Sketch how the mountains have a high-tide line of vegetation, trees surging uphill, rocks spilling down, like waves on an ocean beach. Sort the smells. Sip cool water.

We've caught our breath. We go on.

Views improve as we cross avalanche slides and slopes of talus. Now we see the sawtooth pinnacles. And as we climb, the forest serves as a biologic altimeter, a way to gauge altitude. The valley forest that climaxes in western red cedar, Douglas fir, and western hemlock gives way to yellow cedar and silver fir at three thousand feet, the latter so-named for its silvery, smoother bark. At four thousand to five thousand feet, mountain hemlock begins to dominate, recognizable for its narrow pyramidal shape that sheds deep snow.

Above that, at roughly the 5,392-foot altitude of Cascade Pass, winter reigns, snow and fire opening meadow above tree line. We break into patches of subalpine meadow and subalpine fir, the latter bent by wind into ground-hugging groves called krummholz. Frozen in winter, parched by sun in summer, this zone is difficult for all but the hardiest plants. A whitebark pine six inches in diameter can be four centuries old.

To the east, the mountains slope back down to forests of sub-alpine larch, whitebark pine, Engelmann spruce, Douglas fir, grand fir, and ponderosa pine. We have crested in the middle of a rainbow of ecosystems, contingent on altitude and moisture.

In the last mile of our imaginary hike, we angle up slopes of talus shattered like broken pottery. The bones of the mountains jut out, the mammoth ribs of granite poking through verdant green fur. Corrugated cliffs cast cool shadows, and alpine lakes, blue as lapis lazuli, lurk in cirques left by glaciers.

On top is alpine heaven. Vast fields of bloom erupt in the sun of July and August and then hurry to seed before snow comes. By September the huckleberry is autumn orange, and by October everything is frosted.

The mountains below seem covered in a uniform dark green blanket, but there are actually more than 1,600 species of plant just in North Cascades National Park Complex. We spy purple lupine, puffy clouds of white Sitka valerian, yellow monkey flower, pink phlox that spreads like a carpet, glacier lilies sprouting through the thin snow, heather, and huckleberry. There are wonderfully uncommon common names such as blue-eyed Mary, monkshood, bleeding heart, elephant's-head, pussypaws, bird's-beak lousewort, and dirty socks. Indian paintbrush is flame red, buttercup a cheerful yellow, and Saint-John's-wort as gold as the tantalizing flakes that once lured miners. Even lingering snow patches have life. They catch a fuzz of nutrients like needles, pollen, and lichen and grow watermelon-pink algae.

Meltwater streams weave from one white isle to the next like silver bracelets. Chilly ponds reflect the peaks in peat-colored mirrors. Henry David Thoreau said that a lake is "earth's eye, looking into which the beholder measures the depth of his own nature." Puffy cumulus clouds patrol like Zeppelins. Rocks sparkle.

The peaks here have rounded shoulders about three-quarters of the way up. The last ice age buried this range with snow and ice more than a mile deep. "Morning fog in the southern gorge," wrote poet Philip Whalen from his fire lookout perch on Sauk Mountain in 1953, "gleaming foam restoring the old sea level." Not scientifically accurate—old ice level would be more precise—but a nice capturing of what sculpted this place. The glaciers rasped the ridges. And above this glacial height

head of Lake Chelan and Cascade Pass, counts thirty-seven distinct ecosystems.

In every direction are caps and pinto patches of snow. About 75 percent of the glacier area in the conterminous United States is in Washington State, and 756 glaciers have been counted in the North Cascades, more than 300 of them in North Cascades National Park. (This count, incidentally, is four decades old.) Glaciers outside the park proper include the fifteen on Glacier Peak and eleven on Mount Baker. Each is distinct as a snowflake. They hang, they plow, they melt into lakes to give them a spectacular green or blue tint from ground rock called glacial flour. They shine, and their snouts turn filthy.

In these mountains are enough trail miles to almost reach across the United States: about 400 miles in North Cascades National Park, 1,500 in the Mount Baker–Snoqualmie National Forest, and 1,300 in the Okanogan–Wenatchee National Forest.

Let's perch on a granite boulder and orient ourselves to the North Cascades as a whole.

THE LAY OF THE LAND

Defining the "North Cascades" is a subject of cheerful but earnest debate. While many assume the term is limited to the national park, one historical definition includes all the Cascades north of the Washington–Oregon border. The northern Cascades are in Washington, the southern in Oregon.

But within Washington there is distinction between the granitic peaks in the northern half of the state's range and the lower, more eroded volcanic mountains in the south. This

the peaks rear sharp as knives. Instead of being sanded by ice, they've been splintered by rain, snowmelt, frost heave, earthquake, and avalanche.

Breathe. The atmosphere seems tangible. Blue haze emphasizes the protective envelope of gases keeping us alive. Clouds slide overhead as if blown along a sheet of glass. The sun is brassy, and at night Kerouac's "sizzling stars" are almost touchable.

To the east, we'll descend into quaking aspen and dusty smells like a spice shop. The Stehekin Valley alone, between the northern range is the common ecological definition of the North Cascades, a unified geologic and biologic ecosystem that runs from Interstate 90 to the Fraser River valley in Canada, a distance of about two hundred miles.

The westernmost rampart consists of the snowy cone of Mount Baker and prominent mountains like the Twin Sisters, Whitehorse, Pilchuck, and Si. Within the range, Matterhorn mounts like Index, Baring, Sloan, and Liberty Bell inspire the Swiss comparison.

Some conservationists would extend lands deserving of protection as far west as the Chuckanut foothills of Whatcom and Skagit counties that plunge to saltwater. Their preferred eastern boundary is the Okanogan and Columbia rivers in eastern Washington, including in the North Cascades the rugged Pasayten Wilderness and Canada's Cathedral Peaks. To the north, the range crosses Canada's Highway 3 and takes in Manning Provincial Park.

North Cascades National Park, with 500,936 acres, occupies only the most remote mountains of this vast area. Tightly drawn to make it politically palatable during debates in the 1960s, the park proper is joined to 116,837-acre Ross Lake National Recreation Area and 63,010-acre Lake Chelan National Recreation Area to create a park "complex." The recreation areas permit hunting, dogs, lodges, and motorboats. Adding to the confusion, the Forest Service, not the Park Service, manages the wilderness areas adjacent to this core. "The majority of people we see don't have a clue which agency is which," notes Jon Vanderheyden, a retired district ranger in the Mount Baker–Snoqualmie National Forest. The two most prominent peaks of the North Cascades, the glaciated volcanoes Baker and Glacier, remain in Forest Service wilderness management outside North Cascades National Park.

Historically, there has been no public consensus on which agency's management philosophy is best. The Agriculture Department's Forest Service has permitted logging and mining under a "utilitarian conservation" philosophy, but its lands designated as wilderness remain less developed than most national parks. The Interior Department's popular Park Service, which enjoys recognition similar to NASA or the FBI, has a mission of preserving scenery, natural and cultural objects, and wildlife and providing for their enjoyment by the public. It constructs roads and visitor centers to attract and educate visitors. It too has wilderness lands, however—93 percent of North Cascades National Park Complex is wilderness, and while policies differ slightly on what the two agencies allow, both have become wilderness stewards.

The Mount Baker–Snoqualmie National Forest, encompassing the mountains' western half, has seen its timber harvest decline 90 percent, and its staff and budget slashed in half, since the peak harvest of the late 1980s. "Our priority now is to regrow late-successional [old-growth] habitat," says Vanderheyden. "The road system is going to shrink." Nearly two hundred miles of logging roads have already closed in the forest's Mount Baker District, and the two agencies have moved from rivalry to cooperation.

A succession of wilderness areas protect the alpine core of the Cascades between the national park and Interstate 90, east of Seattle. The most popular is Alpine Lakes, created in 1976. Others are Glacier Peak, 1960; Pasayten, 1968; Boulder River, Mount Baker, Lake Chelan–Sawtooth, Noisy-Diobsud, and Henry M. Jackson, 1984; and Wild Sky, 2008. The region also has a number of logging and farming towns, ski areas, and tourism communities such as Bavarian-themed Leavenworth

Mountain goats in the Enchantments, an area characterized by glaciated mountains ranging from 4,400 feet to 7,800 feet in elevation

Prusik Peak in the Enchantments in the Alpine Lakes Wilderness, in the southern reaches of the North Cascades Ecosystem

and Old West–themed Winthrop. North of the international border, Canada's share of the North Cascades includes, from west to east, Chilliwack Lake, Skagit Valley, E. C. Manning, and Cathedral provincial parks.

In 1969 the US Park Service urged the establishment of parks in Canada along the border, but British Columbia logging interests and American political conservatives opposed it. Nor can US park officials persuade the International Boundary Commission to stop maintaining a twenty-foot-wide swath of clear-cut forest that marks the border along the 49th parallel.

More cooperatively, both countries have collaborated on wildlife research and rehabilitation, fire management, and similar issues. Canadian bears, wolves, and wolverines are "re-wilding" the American North Cascades, notes Mitch Friedman, executive director of the ecosystem advocacy group Conservation Northwest. Particularly intriguing is the grizzly bear, which inhabits the North Cascades north of the international border and drifts southward. Scientists have found tracks and recorded persuasive sightings, including a 2010 hiker photograph, but the number of resident bears on the American side remains unknown. They are reclusive, the backcountry is remote, and the total bear population of the ecosystem is estimated by some bear biologists at no more than thirty to fifty animals. Others estimate even fewer. These omnivores can stand eight feet tall upright and reach six hundred pounds but so far have proved as elusive as Bigfoot to record and study.

One reason tracking is so hard is that the North Cascades are a jumble, twisting like worms and spiking like crabgrass. Two large lakes, however, allow water travel deep inside the range.

On the east, fjord-like Lake Chelan stretches from a point near the Columbia River some fifty-five miles northwest to the Stehekin Valley. The lake has been deepened twenty-one feet by a dam at Chelan but has essentially the same shape as when Indians and explorers canoed it. Chelan is the largest natural lake in Washington and third deepest in the nation, with a depth of 1,486 feet—more than half again as deep as the deepest part of Puget Sound. Its glacier-gouged bottom is 386 feet below sea level, or 104 feet lower than the deepest part of Death Valley. The land rears so steeply out of the cold waters (adjacent Bonanza Peak, the highest non-volcanic mountain in the Cascade Range, is 9,511 feet high) that Chelan is America's deepest gorge, its cliffs so steep that there are few beaches for three-quarters of the lake's length.

Lake Chelan was the first part of the North Cascades to be proposed as a national park, in 1892 and again in 1906, but opposition from mining and land settlement interests squelched that idea. Its northwestern end became a national recreation area when the present park was established in 1968. Yet Lake Chelan and its communities remain the most touristed. *The Belle of Chelan,* the first tourist steamer, was launched in 1889. Excursionists would take the train from Seattle to Wenatchee, a coach to Chelan, and the boat to resort hotels in Stehekin.

Just east of the national park is twenty-four-mile-long Ross Lake, the reservoir behind Ross Dam, which reaches into Canada, with a limited amount of boating and one floating resort. A mile-long trail separates the lake from autos on the North Cascades Highway.

If there is a culminating core to this geography, it is the remote Picket Range east of Mounts Baker and Shuksan. Largely hidden from view from paved roads, the Pickets are punctuated by Mounts Terror, Fury, and Challenger and are accessible only by overnight backpack and then bushwhacking scrambles and climbing.

A loaded kayak awaits its paddler at dusk along the shores of Ross Lake.

The Skagit River runs from high in the Cascade Mountains to Puget Sound. Its floodplain comprises one of the richest agricultural environments in the world, and the region is critical habitat for tens of thousands of migrating snow geese, trumpeter swans, other water fowl, and countless shorebirds.

The biggest river of the range is the Skagit, approximately 150 miles long, originating in Canada and debouching in Skagit Bay. Muscular as a python, its flow is the biggest into Puget Sound and second biggest in the state, after the Columbia–Snake. The Skagit drains 3,130 square miles and is harnessed by three Seattle City Light dams in the heart of the mountains, producing enough electricity for a quarter of Seattle's needs.

At one time the free-flowing river could be canoed from source to the approximate site of today's Ross Dam, where the "ripraps of the Skagit" marked the beginning of its precipitous canyons. The rapids now lie below Ross Lake. The walls of Diablo Lake downstream remain sheer as a skyscraper, reminding us of the original narrow chasm. Measured from riverbed to mountaintop, the cleft that holds Gorge Dam is one of the deepest in the nation, and dark as an alley most of the year.

The dams plugged canyons so narrow that early visitors estimated one bottleneck at only thirteen feet wide, the river shooting through like a fire hose. Salmon could not swim up this gorge, and few people walked. Indian travelers turned at Marblemount to ascend the Cascade River to Cascade Pass, dropping on the other side down to Stehekin (which means "the way through") to canoe Lake Chelan.

Other North Cascades rivers running down to Puget Sound are the Nooksack, Stillaguamish, and the Snoqualmie-Skykomish-Snohomish. On the east side the Okanogan, Methow, Entiat, Chelan, and Wenatchee pour into the Columbia River.

The mountain chain is widest, east to west, at the international border, and just south of the border is twin-fanged Hozomeen, a mountain that haunted Kerouac when he spent two months as a fire lookout on nearby Desolation Peak. Mined by Indians for flint, it is a hypnotic set of horns. "Hozomeen, Hozomeen," Kerouac wrote, "most beautiful mountain I ever seen, like a tiger sometimes with stripes, sunwashed rills and shadow crags wriggling lines in the Bright Daylight, vertical furrows and bumps and Boo!"

ROCKY PILEUP

These mountains' steep ruggedness gives them their unifying nickname as the American Alps, but their rocky bones are anything but simple. Their geologic age ranges from almost zero—marking nineteenth-century eruptions of Baker and eruption at Glacier three hundred years ago—to about 1.6 billion years old, older than the existence of terrestrial animals. The range is a mix of ancient seabed, volcanic action, upthrust granite, and the agglomeration of crust that drifted (possibly from as far away as today's Australia) to "dock" on the edge of North America. The result is a jumbled mass that University of British Columbia geologist Bill Matthews called "the United Plates of America." The Grand Canyon is a tidy layer cake, as readable as a primer. The North Cascades are chaotic jazz.

Hampering our ability to make sense of the pileup is that the entire range has been glaciated multiple times over the last two million years. Each ice age obscured the evidence of earlier ones. At the peak of glaciation, about 30 percent of the earth's land area was covered by ice, compared to 10 percent now. The last ice age was at its maximum about seventeen thousand years ago, when ice at the US–Canadian border was nearly six thousand feet thick, sea level was hundreds of feet lower than now, and gigantic animals like woolly mammoths and saber-toothed cats still roamed North America. The ice began retreating by 13,000 to 14,000 years in the past.

Lake Chelan from along the Chelan Lakeshore Trail. The Lake Chelan National Recreation Area offers abundant recreation opportunities for water sports and hiking.

Smaller climate shifts have since made individual glaciers into yo-yos. A "Little Ice Age" prevailed from the Middle Ages to about 1850, causing glacial advance. But a six-thousand year warming period ending four thousand years ago melted all the glaciers except the highest on Mount Baker and Glacier Peak— and they re-formed later, yet again. The Redoubt Glacier on Redoubt Mountain, near the Canadian border, has advanced and retreated several times in the last eight hundred years. Most recently, glaciers have been in sharp decline, with the Park Service estimating a retreat of about 50 percent in the last century. Since 1910, the total glacial area in the North Cascades, Olympic, and Mount Rainier national parks has shrunk by 13,500 acres.

Annual fluctuation is highly variable, says Park Service geologist Jon Riedel, with North Cascades glaciers accumulating a winter snowpack twenty-five to thirty feet thick that is then lost each summer. In some years, such as the 1998–99 season that saw record snowfall on Mount Baker, the glaciers have a net gain, but more frequently there is a net loss. North Klawatti Glacier, for example, gained mass in seven years between 1993 and 2011 but lost mass in twelve years, for a net reduction.

As the glacial area in the Thunder Creek watershed has declined by almost half, summer streamflow has fallen 30 percent. Coping with such droughts is one of the serious challenges of climate change. Glacial runoff provides 15 to 30 percent of the summer flow of the Skagit River, which is one reason it supports all five species of salmon. Glacial disappearance may make the river less habitable for fish, Riedel says.

Geologists divide the North Cascades into three "domains," or funnel-shaped sections that are widest at the Canadian border and narrow with the range itself. The western domain, west of the Straight Creek Fault that runs through Marblemount, has a good deal of sedimentary rock and of volcanic rock, called igneous. The middle domain, between Marblemount and the Ross Lake Fault, is metamorphic, made up of rocks that have been squeezed and recrystalized at great depth in the earth. The domain east of Ross Lake is more sedimentary, made of shale and sandstones lifted from a shallow sea that once covered eastern Washington.

This explains the volcano domes of Baker and Glacier to the west, the granite crags of the Pickets in the middle, and the rounded and crumbling reddish peaks of the east. Some of the schist, granite, and gneiss of the middle range comes from metamorphic plutons plowing upward from the earth's mantle like sprouting cornstalks, subsequently whittled by wind and water to antler-sharp crags. At Harts Pass, paper-thin layers of shale from the "Methow Ocean" look like leaves of a book.

Unfortunately, this triad fails to represent the complexity of what visitors encounter. Each domain is made up of several "terranes" that represent drifting islands of continental plate that crashed together. So violent and various were these collisions that some beds of rock are not just tilted sideways but stacked in reverse chronological order, putting some of the oldest rocks at the top and some of the youngest on the bottom. This smashup is the result of the westerly drift of North America, which widens the Atlantic and narrows the Pacific at about the rate fingernails grow. As the continent grinds over the seabed floor of the Juan de Fuca Plate, mountains are thrust up, volcanoes roar, and earthquakes shake.

The Twin Sisters, just west of Mount Baker, are made of an olivine dunite, an igneous rock half a billion years old. The

Glacier ice on Mount Baker. Between Snoqualmie Pass and the north boundary of the North Cascades at Mount Garibaldi in British Columbia, there are hundreds of glaciers, many more than the rest of the lower 48 states combined.

The Picket Range in North Cascades National Park. This photograph was taken from the southwest on the shoulder of Bacon Peak.

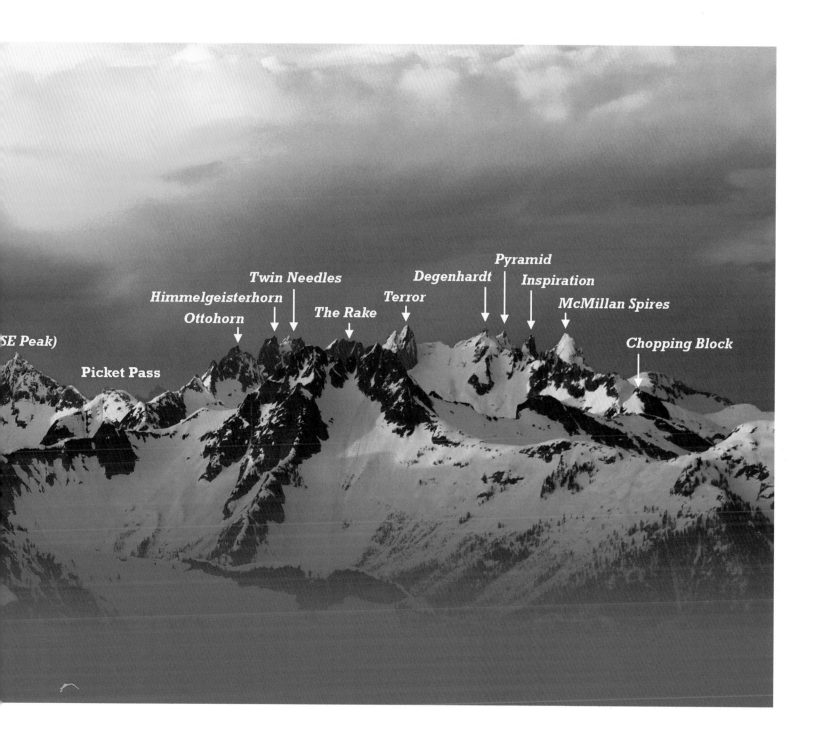

(SE Peak)

Picket Pass

Himmelgeisterhorn

Ottohorn

Twin Needles

The Rake

Terror

Degenhardt

Pyramid

Inspiration

McMillan Spires

Chopping Block

intrusive young volcano now crowds this venerable extrusion stuff, putting some of the North Cascades' oldest rocks next to some of its youngest. Similarly the Black Buttes, on Baker's shoulder, are part of an earlier and bigger volcano that has since eroded and been subsumed by its upstart neighbor.

The Cascades are constantly on the move. A landslide that dammed the Skagit River north of Marblemount and temporarily reversed its course happened a mere 8,400 years ago. Matching rocks on either side of the Straight Creek Fault are as many as sixty-three miles apart, as one side of the fault marched north and the other south, similar to the San Andreas Fault of California.

This drama, still being deciphered by geologists, did have one practical effect: it kept the North Cascades wild. There are no straight passes or easily navigable rivers. Today's spiritual refuge was made possible by a still-restless earth.

WHAT THE MOUNTAINS MEAN TO US

Just as even the rock of the North Cascades is shifting, humans have had an ever-evolving attitude toward mountains. From ancient times through the Renaissance, high places were forbidding, at best the home of the gods and at worst a place of storm, banditry, and wild animals. Jews, Greeks, and Romans thought the perfect roundness of planetary spheres the product of divine geometry, while mountains were a pimple on perfection. Martin Luther preached that the ruggedness of the mountains was evidence of the decay of nature due to human sin. The German Goethe wrote of "the desolation of the ancient hills."

Certainly the North Cascades were daunting. Explorer and army lieutenant John G. Parke, who surveyed the international boundary between 1857 and 1860, wrote that "the entire region is eminently unfit for occupation or settlement."

Others recognized the allure. "No where do the Mountain masses and Peaks present such strange, fantastic, dauntless, and startling outlines as here," wrote Henry Custer in 1859, while surveying the international border. "Whoever wishes to see Nature in all its primitive glory and grandeur, in its almost ferocious wildness, must go and visit these mountain regions."

He was speaking to his era. As the Industrial Revolution took hold and human population exploded from one billion in 1815 to more than seven billion today, mountains were romanticized. ". . . to me, High mountains are a *feeling*," said Childe Harold in Lord Byron's epic poem of 1818.

Henry David Thoreau contended that "in wildness is the preservation of the world." Diplomat and conservationist George Perkins Marsh warned in 1864, after travels in the Mediterranean and Middle East, that ancient civilizations had fallen because of their abuse of the environment. John Muir preached the protection of western landscapes, Aldo Leopold taught the interconnectedness of ecological systems, Rachel Carson warned that the poisons of scientific progress could turn our springs silent of bird call, and Edward Abbey advocated radical resistance to the encroachment of civilization.

National parks evolved to accommodate changing attitudes. They were developed first for the train and then the automobile, becoming what scholar David Louter calls "windshield wilderness." Yet hiking and climbing were advancing at the same time. Portland's Mazamas hiking club and Seattle's Mountaineers led massive groups to the summits of Baker and Glacier. In 1908 the Mountaineers drove a cow to timberline for barbecue slaughter,

Mount Baker at sunset

and in 1910 a Mountaineers party of fifty-seven, more than half of them women, summited Glacier Peak.

Passage of the 1964 Wilderness Act encoded into law the notion that some parts of the United States should remain "untrammeled" by civilization. By the time North Cascades National Park was being legislated in the 1960s, the stage was set for a different kind of national park: wild, unroaded, and hard to get to.

Visionaries began to recognize the North Cascades as a special place at the dawn of the twentieth century, but the initial emphasis was on taming the landscape. "Ecosystem" had not entered the vocabulary. Fire was an enemy. Forestry was an improvement. The wealthy wanted lodges at the edge of the wild.

It was the US Forest Service that established today's trail system to contain fire. In 1897, the federal government set aside 3.6 million acres for the Washington Forest Reserve, transferred to the US Forest Service when the agency was established in 1905, and designated in 1908 as the Washington, Snoqualmie, Chelan, and Wenatchee National Forests. Washington Forest subsequently became the Mount Baker National Forest in 1924.

The agency's first director, Gifford Pinchot, set up a policy of "the greatest good of the greatest number" in deciding what forests were for, and a pattern of "multiple use" as it was later termed, or management that promoted logging in economically accessible parts of the forest and recreation in the remainder. To fulfill its mission, the Forest Service began extending roads, building ranger stations, erecting fire lookouts, and constructing trails to get its personnel within two miles of any likely fire.

The first forestry trail in the Mount Baker area was built in 1904 along Swift Creek. By 1925 there was a trail around Table Mountain, and in 1935 surveying began for a Cascade Crest Trail. Meanwhile, in 1927 investors constructed Mount Baker Lodge, where the ski area is today. It had one hundred rooms, a seventy-foot observation tower, miniature golf, and pony rides and drew 11,700 guests its first year. It burned in 1931, however, and the Depression prevented reconstruction.

The early rangers were rugged outdoorsmen. One recruit, John Barber, was called "the Daniel Boone of Blaine." They had to camp, pack, and survive. An early agency test for prospective employees required them to identify ten tree species, describe how to bake biscuits over a fire, pack a horse, use a seven-foot crosscut saw, and pace a triangle of land and compute its acreage. One famed challenge was falling a tree at least ten inches in diameter with such accuracy that it would drive a stake into the ground. Only one applicant in sixteen managed to cut with such finesse, but small wonder that the cadre developed esprit de corps.

They were stewards of a vast ecosystem only barely understood. Many of the more than three hundred species of mammal, bird, and fish in the future park were still unrecognized. The ecological role of predators, the forest health provided by biological diversity, the importance of ecosystem connections that allow animals to move from one region to another, the nourishing effects of migrating salmon, and the rehabilitating effects of fire were all unknown.

But it was the rangers who opened the wonderland, and with trail building came naming. Wenatchee Forest supervisor Albert Sylvester supplied more than one thousand names, many imaginative and evocative. It was Sylvester who gave the name Enchantment Lakes to that exquisite alpine destination in the early twentieth century. Later, hikers Bill and Peg Stark of Leavenworth used Norse mythology and fairy lore to name features such as the Leprechaun, Sprite, Gnome, Crystal, Temple, Freya, and Valhalla lakes and tarns. Reached via a challenging trail with more than a vertical mile of elevation gain, the lakes are in the spectacular eighty-million plus-year-old Stuart Range, which can be viewed from afar at the Indian John Hill rest stop on Interstate 90 near Cle Elum.

Other names were whimsical. Choral and Anthem Creeks "sung," Overcoat Peak was where Sylvester left a too-small overcoat buttoned around his cairn, and Dishpan Gap was named for a rusty dishpan found there. After naming Labyrinth Mountain for its complex contours, Sylvester christened Minotaur and Theseus lakes.

The Forest Service's primary mission in the North Cascades was defined in 1926 by the Big Beaver Creek and Bacon Creek fires, which burned about 50,000 acres. Here was unruly nature, begging for discipline from humankind. No matter that four hundred men had been unable to put the fires out, or that the blazes weren't extinguished until October snow. Nor that fire after fire followed this pattern; extinguished by autumn instead of by smoke jumpers. Combatting fire gave the Forest Service a cause taxpayers could understand. To fight fires you had to find them, so more than six hundred mountaintop lookouts were built in Washington. Forty-three of these were in the Mount Baker Forest. Statewide, almost 90 percent have since been removed.

Lookout season was lonely, hermetic, and blessedly short. In 1952, when future poet Gary Snyder was assigned to 8,128-foot Crater Mountain just southeast of Ross Lake (the peak so named because it appears a bite was taken out of the top), he had just five weeks between the time snow had melted enough to reach the shelter, until new snow arrived at the end of August. It took the Seattle and Portland native a week to winch his seasonal supply of food up the last precipitous pitch to the lookout. Then, once the summit snow melted away, he had to make daily hikes down to Jerry Glacier to chip off ice, load it in his backpack, and carry it back to melt and drink.

Ah, but what a view! Snyder called the sea of peaks that he could survey on a clear day "a perfection of chaos." He was investigating Buddhism at the time and festooned the lookout with

Hannegan Pass and Ruth Mountain in the Mount Baker–Snoqualmie National Forest

prayer flags. Rare visitors, all male, would be greeted by a nut-brown seasonal employee wearing nothing but a jockstrap and hiking boots, jotting down observations for future books. His poetry, some of it inspired by this experience, won a Pulitzer Prize in 1975.

Snyder was one of at least seven notable writers drawn to the North Cascades. In the early 1900s, Owen Wister visited Winthrop on the east end of today's North Cascades Highway and incorporated his observations into his classic Western, *The Virginian.* In 1924, future San Francisco poetry dean Kenneth Rexroth worked on a trail crew out of Marblemount. He became a nexus of the San Francisco Beat movement of the 1950s. Poet Philip Whalen, from Portland, occupied the lookout on Sauk Mountain. Massachusetts native Jack Kerouac was persuaded by his literary pals to have a go at the lookout on Desolation Peak. Contemporary poet Tim McNulty also worked as a fire lookout. Tobias Wolff, who was raised in Newhalem and attended school in Concrete, recalled his foothills childhood in *This Boy's Life.*

"There's a different kind of literature that comes out of these mountains," says the North Cascades Institute's Saul Weisberg, another poet of the peaks. It is mystic, contemplative, and celebratory.

Kerouac, who already had the drinking problem that would kill him, apparently went drug and alcohol free during his sixty-three days on Desolation. He couldn't survive without smoking, however, and hiked 4,400 vertical feet down to Ross Lake to get a tin of tobacco from a Forest Service boat, just two weeks into his stay. While Snyder and Whalen found Buddhist serenity in the wilderness, Kerouac's thinly fictionalized autobiography of this time is one of awe, appreciation, loneliness, unease, and fear. Here was solitude buffeted by lightning and shrouded by

clouds. He missed civilization. He missed people. It was a place of snowstorms in July, thunderbolt strikes, brewing forest fires, and solar radiation, hot by day and frozen by night. It was the world made raw.

While the poets accumulated impressions of wilderness, human development accelerated. Surveys to harness the waterpower of the mighty Skagit began in 1907, and construction of the first Gorge Dam was underway by 1919. Each generation has brought its own idealism to the mountains: damming the Skagit was a way to take control of electricity away from private power companies and give it to publicly managed utilities.

The first wooden Gorge Dam was replaced by a concrete structure and then by today's higher concrete dam, and it took decades to work out all the kinks in its powerhouse and generators. Next upriver was Diablo Dam. When completed in 1930, the 389-foot dam was the highest thin arch dam in the world. But the real power producer was Ross Dam. By 1949 it had reached a height of 540 feet, its reservoir flooding twenty-four miles of valley that had been filled with virgin timber, and its power pylons each a silver colossus with swooping wires. No North Cascades project has been more controversial. Environmental activist and author Harvey Manning wrote that Ross Dam "wreaked more destruction of natural wonders in the North Cascades than all the other dammers, all the highwaymen, all the dirty miners, and half the loggers combined."

But in the 1930s Seattle City Light became masterful in promoting the project, taking up to 1,500 tourists a week on elaborate tours with an overnight stay, generous meals, and a sound-and-light show behind the Gorge Powerhouse at Ladder Falls. As rainbow colors played on the plunging waters (which were undammed), heroic music played from loudspeakers in

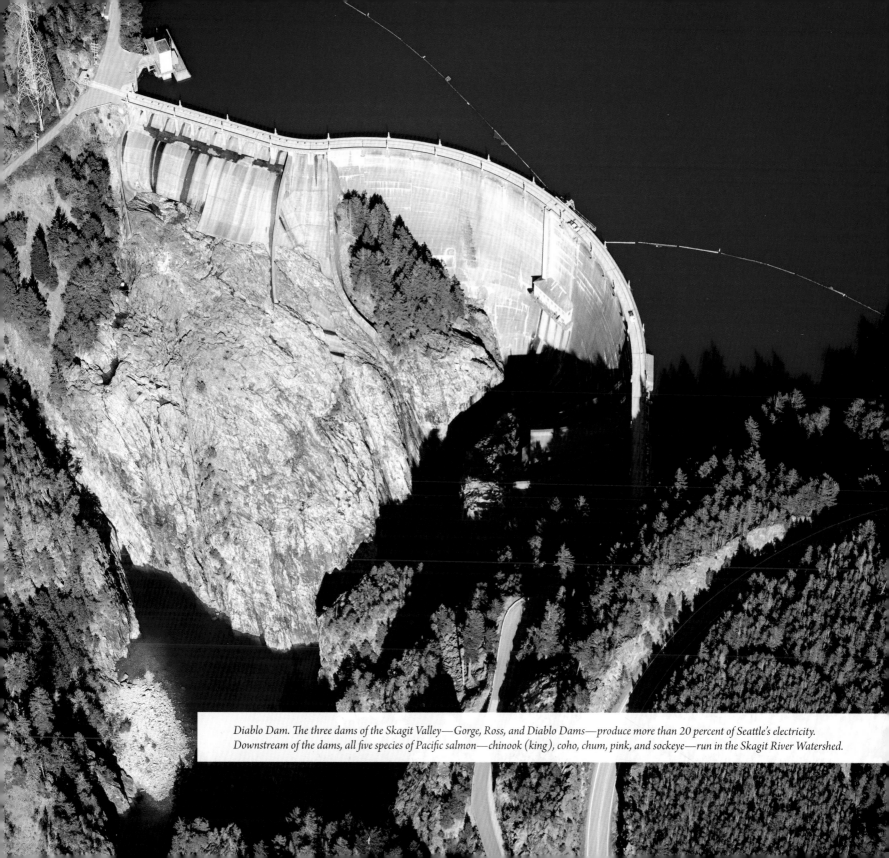

Diablo Dam. The three dams of the Skagit Valley—Gorge, Ross, and Diablo Dams—produce more than 20 percent of Seattle's electricity. Downstream of the dams, all five species of Pacific salmon—chinook (king), coho, chum, pink, and sockeye—run in the Skagit River Watershed.

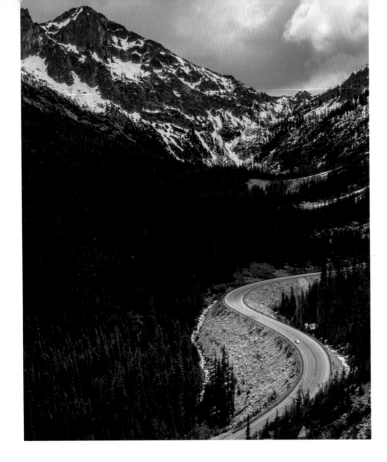

North Cascades Scenic Highway (State Route 20) below Washington Pass

the trees. The tours are no longer so dramatic, but they remain popular today.

Still, attitudes shifted. By 1967, when the utility reached an agreement with Canada to allow the flooding which would result from elevating Ross Dam another 125 feet, the environmental movement pulsed with its own power. In the same year that North Cascades National Park was created, Seattle proposed to flood 7.4 more square miles of important wetlands and forests in British Columbia and groves of giant western red cedars in the United States. Opposition rose quicker than a dam reservoir level, and years of studies, hearings, and protest followed. Canada joined the objectors.

By 1984, the two countries had agreed to abandon the higher dam idea. This was followed by additional battles over dam

relicensing from the US government and resulted in 1991 in City Light agreeing to spend $100 million on mitigation for the environmental impacts of the original reservoirs. Included was $17 million to purchase more than four thousand acres of wildlife habitat and $9 million to replace the abandoned Diablo Lake Resort with a new Environmental Learning Center run by the nonprofit North Cascades Institute.

The institute, founded in 1986 by Saul Weisberg and colleagues, was symbolic of the rapid evolution of public thought. These were mountains that could teach an increasingly frenetic civilization, and the institute's programs for children and adults proved as popular as dam tours. The Environmental Learning Center, ultimately costing almost $12 million and opening in 2005, is a three-way partnership. City Light owns the buildings, the National Park Service owns and manages the lands, and the institute administers the environmental programs. Set on the glacial green waters of Diablo Lake at the foot of Sourdough Mountain, the LEED-designed facility looks across to Pyramid Peak and provides today's overnight visitors a stunning and soothing experience in the heart of the mountains.

Such experiences are a product of progressive intent by visionary individuals over many decades. Bills were introduced as early as 1916 to make Mount Baker a national park. They didn't pass, but the idea of preservation wouldn't go away. The North Cascades were being eyed simultaneously for hydroelectric power, timber, gold, recreation, and preservation.

The questions became, and have remained, Whose mountains are these? What are mountains for?

THE WILDEST OF PARKS

European settlement of the United States began with the nation's land unclaimed and unexplored by the newcomers. Then it was owned by the government and then partly distributed to private landowners through sale, grant, and homestead. The process left most of the land east of the Mississippi in private ownership, but in the West and Alaska, vast tracts of public and highly scenic mountainous terrain remained public as the conservation ethic grew. California's Yosemite Valley was set aside as a state park in 1864 (later national, in 1890), and Yellowstone became the first national park in 1872.

John Muir founded the Sierra Club in 1892, and the National Park Service was created in 1916. In Washington, Mount Rainier became the first park created from a national forest, in 1899. Olympic National Park followed in 1938, over the objection of many peninsula residents.

Our idea of "park" has steadily evolved. Railroads initially saw parks as an enticement to draw people west, using their lines to transport tourists to grand lodges. The early Park Service saw visitation as key to its institutional survival and turned to the automobile as a way to unite humans with nature. Historian David Louter quotes a 1920s park service brochure that called circling Oregon's Crater Lake by car "a spiritual experience—nothing less."

Mount Rainier National Park was the first park to officially admit automobiles, in 1908, and was developed to allow a near circumnavigation of the peak by car. With alpine parking lots at Paradise and Sunrise, the sky was literally the limit. In 1911, Assistant Secretary of the Interior Carmi A. Thompson promised to support a road all the way to the top! While that was unrealistic, trams were suggested as well.

The history of national park development is long, complex, and contentious. Today, eighty-four million acres are divided into 401 separate areas under the control of the Park Service, including not just parks but preserves, monuments, memorials, historic sites, seashores, lakeshores, battlefields, wild and scenic rivers, national scenic trails, national recreation areas, and national parkways. Parks can be as developed as the Old Faithful area of Yellowstone and the South Rim of the Grand Canyon, or as remote as Gates of the Arctic in Alaska's Brooks Range. Yosemite Village in Yosemite Valley, on a peak summer day, endures a population density equal to that of Los Angeles County.

The North Cascades are, and were, different. A 1938 highway map of Washington is striking for the absence of roads north of Stevens Pass, depicting a cornucopia of remote wilderness opening toward Canada. The Sierra Club recognized this geographic rarity in the 1950s and advocated for a wilderness park with brochures, books, and movies. Seattle organizations joined in. Hikes were organized and lectures made.

At the same time, small-town boosters on both sides of the range clamored for a highway between the Skagit Valley on the west and the Methow Valley on the east. By 1972, both sides would have their wish.

For most people, the North Cascades today are divided, and made accessible, by road. Interstate 90 marks the southern boundary and crosses over Snoqualmie Pass, 3,022 feet in elevation. This freeway was originally converted from a trail to a wagon road in 1868, transited by the first automobile in 1905, and then steadily expanded by state and federal highway engineers beginning in 1926. It is still being widened, but also bridged to allow animals to cross.

To the north US Highway 2, crossing 4,056-foot Stevens Pass, was open all year and paved or oiled from Wenatchee to Everett by 1950. State Route 20 (the North Cascades Highway) crossed 4,855-foot Rainy Pass and 5,477-foot Washington Pass in 1972. Canada's Highway 3, the Crowsnest Highway, crossed 4,403-foot Allison Pass in the northernmost range in 1932.

Other roads branch into the mountains. In Washington they include the Mountain Loop Highway in Snohomish County, between Granite Falls (where it starts out as State Route 92) and Darrington (where it ends as State Route 530); US Highway 97 over 4,102-foot Blewett Pass that skirts the eastern slopes between Ellensburg and Canada; and the Mount Baker Highway (State Route 542), which culminates at mile-high Artist Point. This last road is so snowy that the top is typically open only between July and September, and some years it does not open at all.

Near Leavenworth, branch roads lead from US Highway 2 to sky-blue Lake Wenatchee and Icicle Creek. The Baker Lake Road from State Route 20 takes visitors to trails and campgrounds on the east side of Mount Baker. Farther up the Skagit Valley at Marblemount, the part gravel Cascade River Road provides the only motorized access into the edge of North Cascades National Park. And on the east side of the Cascade Crest, the Harts Pass gravel road reaches the highest point served by road in Washington, at 7,440-foot Slate Peak.

There is a twenty-three-mile road up the Stehekin Valley, of which only the first four miles are paved. At this writing, all but the first thirteen miles are closed because of repeated flood damage. Debate continues on whether to repair any of the closed section and how much to permanently close.

Canada's graveled Silver–Skagit Road follows the upper Skagit Valley to the upper end of Ross Lake, at the US–Canadian border. A gravel road also winds through Cathedral Provincial Park. There is a private, gated road there that takes guests to Canada's highest hotel at 6,800 feet, Cathedral Lakes Lodge on Quiniscoe Lake.

Added to these major routes are thousands of miles of Forest Service logging roads that crisscross the lower peaks.

All these roads, developed over the last hundred years, define most people's experience of the mountains. None represent a master plan, but are rather a grab bag of dreams, ambitions, and expedience that present opportunities and problems. Should America's Alps be as heavily developed as their Swiss counterpart, should they vie for Alaska-like isolation, or should they remain a median in-between?

Past development plans have been ambitious. There were proposals for a road encircling Mount Baker and for aerial trams up Mount Shuksan, Colonial Peak, Arctic Creek, and Ruby Mountain. Proponents reasoned that trams were an ecologically sensible, low-polluting, and democratic way to get sightseers to the view.

There were proposals for a car ferry on Ross Lake to take visitors between the dam and the head of the lake in Canada. The face of Ross Dam itself has a waffle-iron pattern to tie in new concrete if it had been raised 125 feet as planned. Had that happened, there was to be a huge parking lot and recreational access off of the North Cascades Highway.

Over time, there have been proposals to clear-cut the Stehekin Valley, to build a major downhill ski area at Early Winters near Mazama, to develop an open-pit copper mine on

Laying track on Bridge No. 1 on Stevens Pass

The "Sunset Highway" near Snoqualmie Pass, circa 1920

the southeast side of Glacier Peak, and to log Glacier's forested valleys to tree line.

Logging in Washington began at saltwater to provide lumber for the California gold rush starting in 1848, but several inventions pushed harvest toward the mountains. The steam donkey, patented in 1882, replaced oxen and horses as a means to drag logs across steep terrain. Logging railroads were pushed up North Cascades river valleys beginning in the late nineteenth century, and almost all of the low-elevation flatland was cleared of old growth. The logging truck followed after World War II, allowing roads to be built in the foothills that trains couldn't penetrate. The chainsaw, which originated in the 1920s but was not in wide use until the start of World War II, accelerated the cut. Harvest went from somewhat more than a billion board feet per year in 1890 to over seven billion by the late 1920s. (A board foot is a unit of wood a foot square and an inch thick.) While that harvest peak was never exceeded—total statewide harvest peaked again at seven billion board feet in 1987 and fell to four billion by 2000—logging on the more remote Forest Service lands was highest in the late 1980s. By this time environmentalists were raising an outcry and enlisting science to protect the endangered spotted owl.

A century of logging left a patchwork of clear-cuts and regrowing second growth on Cascade foothills, with most surviving "late successional" forest confined to higher slopes. Hundreds of miles of logging roads led to erosion. Suburban sprawl and agriculture has decreased the state's total forest land by about 1.4 million acres since the 1970s. North Cascades National Park and the surrounding wilderness areas were designed to preserve some remnants of ancient forest, but since adoption of the 1994 Northwest Forest Plan, forest outside those boundaries is also being managed to regain old-growth characteristics. Without clear federal protection, those policies will have to be sustained for decades, or even centuries, to succeed and begin to restore the original ecosystem.

In sum, very little of the wilderness preserved in today's mountains "just happened." It was saved by way of controversy and campaigns. In the late 1950s, Sierra Club leader David Brower led thirteen outings to the North Cascades, with seven hundred participants, to promote the preservation of Glacier Peak as wilderness. The club printed 125,000 brochures and 350,000 postcards. On the opposing side, the commissioners of Whatcom, Skagit, Okanogan, and Chelan counties all fought the creation of North Cascades National Park.

The twenty-first-century challenge for the North Cascades is to achieve public consensus on the evolving ethic for these peaks. Judging from the region's history, that will not be easy.

Causes sometimes coalesce around a name. The invention of "ancient forest" gave a catchier description for "old growth," "virgin," or "late successional" timber and succeeded in capturing the public imagination, leading to a Northwest Forest Plan that sharply curtailed logging on federal land. Similarly, conservationists coined the terms "wilderness Alps" or "American Alps" to describe the North Cascades in the 1950s and 1960s, elevating a little-known American region to the status of a foreign landscape that Americans were more familiar with from photographs and movies. The implication was that if the United States had a mountain range of *Sound of Music* glory, it indeed deserved protection. The Stehekin Valley became "the Yosemite of the North."

"The problem of the North Cascades was that they did not stare much of anybody in the face, as the Olympics and Rainier did,"

850. A Washington Log.

This postcard celebrates loggers, who cut enormous trees by hand using axes and crosscut saws during the early pioneer logging boom in the Pacific Northwest.

wrote Harvey Manning, editor and publisher of the journal of the North Cascades Conservation Council. Words were important.

So were changing times. Postwar prosperity brought middle-class America into the nation's wildernesses and parks. Improved equipment made camping and hiking more comfortable. Baby boomers unleashed a torrent of recreationists into the mountains in the 1960s and 1970s. All these changes set up a collision of values, and the environmental movement vowed to preserve the last, best places. When North Cascades and Redwood national parks were established by law in 1968, they were the first big parks in the American West since Olympic in 1938 and Canyonlands in 1964.

Preservation of the North Cascades came in steps. In 1926 the federal government designated a 74,859-acre recreation area around Mount Baker. A larger acreage of game preserves established by the state followed, and then in 1931 came a Glacier Peak–Cascade Recreation Unit of 233,600 acres. Also in 1931

came the Whatcom Primitive Area, superseded by the 801,000-acre North Cascades Primitive Area in 1935.

While early suggestions for national parks around Baker, Glacier, and Lake Chelan went nowhere, by 1937 these ideas had been superseded by an "Ice Peaks National Park" proposal that would have stretched from the Canadian border to within twenty-five miles of the Columbia River. It would have included all five of Washington's volcanoes. Mining and logging interests quickly defeated the idea, but much of what was proposed is protected in parks and wilderness areas today.

World War II interrupted campaigns for preservation, but postwar immigration of activists from the Bay Area to Seattle forged ties between conservationists on Puget Sound and those in San Francisco. This helped make protection of the North Cascades a national as well as local cause.

The devil was in the details. Where to draw lines? Which agency? What rules? Environmentalists initially were offered only a "wilderness on the rocks," or preservation of alpine areas

so high, remote, and snowy that they had no possible economic use. Advocates then sought to push the boundary lines to save the forested valleys. In many cases the conservation community was unsuccessful, and one of the key issues now is restoring a coherent ecosystem by preserving or restoring lowland forests and wetlands.

By 1957, leading Seattle conservationists decided to launch a new organization focusing on the North Cascades, and the North Cascades Conservation Council (NCCC) was born. Phil Zalesky of Everett was president; Patrick Goldsworthy of Seattle, first vice president; Una Davies of Oswego, Oregon, second vice president; Polly Dyer of Seattle was corresponding secretary; Neva Karrick of Seattle was recording secretary; and Yvonne Prater of Ellensburg was treasurer. Many would play key roles for decades to come. In 1963, NCCC consultant Mike McCloskey produced an influential 120-page prospectus outlining a proposed park.

The first campaign, however, was for a wilderness around Glacier Peak. The regional press and traditional business interests were initially opposed. But the extractive West was giving way to highly educated urbanites anxious for outdoor experience. Environmentalists generated a steady campaign of sympathetic national press stories, organized hikes for power brokers, and circulated spectacular pictures. In his classic *Encounters with the Archdruid, New Yorker* writer John McPhee depicted a sharp debate, during a wilderness hike, between the Sierra Club's David Brower and Charles Park, a mineral geologist advocating an open-pit copper mine next to the icy volcano. The Glacier Peak Wilderness east of the logging town of Darrington was established by the Forest Service in 1960 and expanded in 1968 and 1984. Meanwhile a national Wilderness Act was passed in 1964, giving a concrete legislative foundation to earlier Forest Service designations like Glacier.

Seeking to define "wilderness," Howard Zahniser of the Wilderness Society took the suggestion of the NCCC's Dyer that "untrammeled" captured what environmentalists were trying to get across. Zahniser's definition thus became, "A wilderness, in contrast with those areas where man and his own works dominate the landscape, is hereby recognized as an area where the earth and its community of life are untrammeled by man, where man himself is a visitor who does not remain." As anthropological research revealed that the North Cascades had been trammeled for almost ten millennia, and that man's impacts today can include global warming or invasive species, trying to pin down "wilderness" has became more difficult, but consensus holds that it remain undeveloped.

With Glacier protected, next up was a national park. Support came from not just the NCCC but the Sierra Club, Wilderness Society, The Mountaineers, Spokane Mountaineers, and the National Parks Association. KING-TV's Stimson Bullitt was a member of the NCCC and encouraged early television stories. The *Seattle Times*, initially skeptical, joined in on the print side. Political leaders included Washington's Governor Dan Evans, Senator Henry Jackson, and Congressman Lloyd Meeds.

In retrospect, the campaign for North Cascades National Park seems emblematic of wider struggle. The decade-long campaign from 1958 to 1968 coincided with one of the most turbulent periods in American history. There were the Kennedy and King assassinations, the civil rights movement, Vietnam, the race to the moon, Beatlemania, *Silent Spring*, the Cold War, the counterculture, and the rise of feminism. Attitudes about everything were a-changin', including those about our planet and our place on it. Less than three months after the North Cascades bill was signed, astronaut William Anders snapped a picture of the earth rising over the barren moon that nature photographer Galen Rowell called "the most influential environmental photo ever taken." The Industrial Revolution was giving way to a postindustrial information economy. The Environmental Protection Agency was created and the Clean Air Act passed in 1970. The Clean Water Act followed in 1972. The new park was not just a sign of the times. It was a result.

Conservation group proposals for preservation of the North Cascades were supplemented by agency proposals in the 1960s, and much horse trading ensued. The initial National Park Service proposal included two parks that would encompass the two most prominent peaks, Baker and Glacier. The Forest Service, not wanting to lose any land to a rival agency, countered with no park at all, but instead a network of wilderness and recreation areas. Washington senator Henry Jackson put forth a different idea—shrinking the Olympic National Park boundaries in return for a new park in the North Cascades—but it didn't fly. Jackson also defused opposition in the US House of Representatives by removing his opposition to the Central Arizona Project (a mammoth water-diversion scheme) desired by Congressman Wayne Aspinall. As the bargaining accelerated, there were proposals for a new network of "scenic roads" throughout the North Cascades. Counterbalancing this were ideas for an Alpine Lakes Wilderness and new wilderness lands around Mount Rainier.

On the broadest scale, environmentalists, industry, agencies, and politicians were resolving controversies that had been developing since pioneer days. The lowlands were for human development, the highest country would be preserved, but the knotty question was where to draw the line. How many richly timbered valleys should be protected from logging? How much epic scenery should be opened to easy access by the automobile? Which lands would allow hunting, fishing, snowmobiling, skiing, dogs, and horses? Which communities would wind up as commercial gateways to recreational playgrounds? Millions of acres and billions of dollars were at stake.

Three different bills were introduced in Congress and passionate hearings were held. The Seattle audience was overwhelmingly in favor of a park, while local communities were almost unanimously opposed. The result was a conservation triumph, but a compromise on several fronts.

First, the new park was split in half by the national recreation area corridor holding the new North Cascades Highway, allowing state plans to proceed without federal interference. A Park Service road, former park superintendent Chip Jenkins notes, would likely have been slower, narrower, and more scenic, better for sightseers and worse for truckers and travelers.

Second, Mount Baker and Glacier Peak—both proposed for park status from an early date—were left out. To stand at Artist Point and realize that Mount Shuksan in one direction is inside the park, and Mount Baker in the other is not, is testament to the oddities of compromise. The existing park is a relatively narrow wedge of the North Cascades, excluding not only the volcanoes to the west but most of the mountains traversed by the Pacific Crest National Scenic Trail to the east. The splendid panorama from the Washington Pass Overlook, next to Liberty Bell

Iconic features of the North Cascades, including Early Winters Spires, Liberty Bell Mountain (high in the Stehekin River watershed), and beyond to Tower Mountain and Golden Horn (high in the Skagit River watershed) lie in a Roadless Area. However, they lack permanent legislative protection as Wilderness.

An old logging road in a drainage of the Chilliwack River in British Columbia close to the international boundary

Mountain, is entirely outside the park. So are Crater Mountain, where poet Gary Snyder once watched for fires, and glacier-clad Mount Formidable and Dome Peak.

Third, the park would be entirely different than Mount Rainier in that it would remain wilderness. No lodges, almost no roads, and no museums within the park itself. The visitor center and Ross Lake Resort are in the recreation corridor, not the park.

Fourth, the park was bisected by three dam reservoirs. Boundaries were drawn in 1968 so that Ross Dam, if raised, could still drown the Big Beaver Valley, a tunnel could divert Thunder Creek to Ross Lake, and the Cascade River valley could still be logged.

North Cascades was thus the wildest of parks and also the most constricted, the most visionary of parks and the most compromised. It was the nexus of a colossal sea of wilderness and yet invisible from the region's major urban centers.

Economics broke the preservationist way. The core of the mountains did not have the mineral bonanza that prospectors had hoped for and was a difficult place to harvest trees and regrow them. Globalization and mechanization enormously changed the Northwest timber industry, and today much of it concentrates on high-productivity, low-elevation tree farms with efficient mills and a much smaller labor base. It became politically safer to champion wilderness. The reversion of federal timberlands toward old-growth forest under the Northwest Forest Plan of 1994 has resulted in a de facto expansion of North Cascades ecosystem boundaries and has put the goals of the Forest Service and Park Service in closer alignment.

On the other end of the scale, the completion of the North Cascades Highway in 1972 and the thirty-year relicensing of the Skagit River dams in the 1990s and fifty-year relicensing of the Baker River dams in 2008 cast into concrete North Cascades developments that satisfy commercial interests.

Recent decades have also seen the North Cascades evolve to host a wide range of recreational experiences. The national park and adjacent wilderness remain accessible primarily to hikers and climbers. But the national recreational areas within the complex, and Forest Service lands outside it, provide campgrounds and boat launches. Resort towns like Suncadia, Leavenworth, Mazama, and Winthrop provide lodges and motels within easy reach of trails. Manning and Cathedral provincial parks in British Columbia provide lodges, and Manning has a highly developed campground complex. There are half a dozen ski areas in the North Cascades, and opportunities for canoeing, kayaking, rafting, trail running, mountain biking, rock climbing, hunting, and fishing are numerous. Moreover, the range is near other national, state, and provincial parks. Enthusiasts may debate which share each recreation group gets, but the decades of debate have resulted in both an intact ecosystem and a multiplicity of uses.

Adjustments will continue. Demographers forecast that by midcentury, there will be a considerably higher percentage of elderly Americans than of children. What will the politics of aging do to wilderness debate?

ROADS, TOWNS, AND TOURISTS

By 1970, early park plans still called for an aerial tram, High Ross Dam, a spur road to Ross Lake with a lodge and boat launch, a car ferry to Hozomeen in Canada, and scenic boat trips. Environmentalists opposed all these, and none came to pass.

What did happen was the North Cascades Highway. Proposals for a road through the heart of the range date back to 1893, but

Above: *Bicycle riders on the seasonally closed North Cascades Highway enjoy a remote wilderness road without concern for traffic—but they may face other hazards such as this spring avalanche debris that has fallen onto the highway off the northern slopes of Ruby Mountain. Below: Cars drive Highway 20 over Washington Pass, below Liberty Bell and the Early Winters Spires.*

mapping was so murky that the routes suggested didn't even exist. As geographic knowledge improved, a dozen different possibilities were eventually studied. The route was called at various times the Skagit River Road, the Methow–Barron Road, the Roosevelt Highway, the North Cross-State Highway, and finally the North Cascades Highway.

The most common suggestion was a route following the Indian trail up the Cascade River, over Cascade Pass, and down the Stehekin Valley. Rather than dead-end at the precipitous cliffs of Lake Chelan, the highway would angle from the Stehekin River to Washington Pass by way of Bridge Creek and then descend to Mazama and Winthrop. An alternate route to the north would have ascended to Harts Pass by Ruby, Canyon, and Slate creeks, again descending to the Methow River. Both passes are high and precipitous, however, and engineers were dubious.

In 1932, highway location engineer Ivan "Ike" Munson suggested the route that was finally followed. The highway would hug Diablo Lake to Ross Dam and then ascend Granite Creek to Rainy and Washington passes. This was not easy either—the ascent up Liberty Bell Mountain to Washington Pass required a wide swooping S pummeled by avalanches each winter—but a 1956 pack-train trip along the route convinced state officials. One who rode along was orchardist George Zahn, who became chairman of the state's Highway Commission and the road's most zealous apostle. He found the money for construction and died just one year before the final opening in 1972.

By the early 1960s, bulldozers were at work on both ends of the new highway, and by 1964 only thirty miles separated the work crews. It was a highway built for speed, not contemplation, justified to move commodities. The minerals, timber, and farm goods projected never materialized, however, and it remains primarily a tourist highway today.

Governor Dan Evans led a four-wheel-drive procession on the highway's pilot road in 1968, the same year the park was created. Paving followed. On September 2, 1972, grand-opening ceremonies were held in Winthrop, Newhalem, and Sedro-Woolley. Serial killer Ted Bundy, a charmer then working as a political aide, later claimed he'd chauffeured Evans's car at the head of the cross-mountain procession and thus was the first man to drive the North Cascades Highway. Evans later denied the claim as nonsense, although Bundy probably did ride somewhere in the stream of more than one hundred vehicles that day.

The highway has been hailed as a paragon of sensitive engineering and condemned as a travesty that spilled excavation debris into virgin forest and pristine creeks. The National Society of Professional Engineers recognized it as a major achievement, while activist and author Harvey Manning called it "a boondoggle" and "needless."

On either side of the highway, North Cascades National Park took over the complex job of managing a sprawling landscape with a long history of human use. In the 1970s, the park examined and invalidated thousands of mining claims that had never been developed and spent $6 million buying out twenty-one additional tracts totaling 1,435 acres. A few private inholdings remain.

The 1950s era of "poets on the peaks" ended. Aircraft superseded fire lookouts and fire came to be seen as a necessary part of the ecological cycle. More frequent fires consume fuel loads and don't burn as hot, sparing many trees. Fire suppression, in contrast, allows dead branches and needles to build up and sets the stage for catastrophic blazes.

Established in 1989, Stehekin Pastry Company is a community hub.

The federal government moved away from early North Cascades development ideas. Congress passed a 1988 bill designating almost all of North Cascades, Mount Rainier, and Olympic national parks as wilderness. That means a total of 634,614 acres in North Cascades National Park Service Complex and 1.7 million acres in the three parks combined. The new emphasis is on stewardship, education, and restoration.

A major effort has been made to restore denuded meadow areas overrun by backpackers, and the park preference is to permanently close the upper ten miles of the Stehekin Valley Road closed after portions were washed away in 1995, 2003, and 2006 floods. At this writing, legislation is pending in Congress concerning this closed length of road. Two miles of road in the Lower Stehekin Valley (that is, down valley from High Bridge) will be rerouted beginning in 2015, with a spur to McGregor Meadows, and paving to nine miles from Stehekin Landing, at a cost of $10 million.

It is rare to have an existing hamlet drawn inside a national recreation area that is an extension of a national park, and the Park Service's relationship with Stehekin has been knotty. The small wilderness community at the head of Lake Chelan didn't even have widely available electricity until after World War II and prided itself on its independence and isolation. By 1980, the Park Service spent about $2.4 million acquiring about nine hundred private acres in the valley from willing buyers, and it acquired and consolidated three lodges at the lake edge.

Stehekin has since evolved from homestead and mining village to a community in which the largest employer is the National Park Service. It has built a tourist industry sustained by the boat *Lady of the Lake* and other boats and aircraft. Entire books could be written about the history and management controversies of this colorful community, and several have been. Suffice it to say that issues of road maintenance, tourist management, firewood cutting, airstrip use, and wilderness access continue to simmer.

So what now?

THE FUTURE OF CONSERVATION

As magnificent as the view is from the mountain crest of our earlier virtual hike, we won't linger. Clouds are darkening to the west, the wind is rising, and the temperature drops. Even on a fine summer day, the mountains tolerate our presence more than embrace it. We ramble toward the drier country to the east, passing the dirty blue snout of a glacier and the silver mirror of a lake. Thunder growls, and there is a scent of ozone in the air. We feel urgency to pitch a safe camp, just as the press of population in the hazy lowlands gives urgency to decisions about the North Cascades.

As hikers tramp into the twenty-first century and families continue to spread their big blue tarps in the campgrounds, there is a growing feeling that our stewardship of this region remains uncompleted, despite the astonishing protection of 2.7 million acres in the overall range. The North Cascades have never seemed more threatened, or more precious. Global issues have overtaken regional ones. The visionaries who first proposed preservation of this magnificent wilderness couldn't imagine that industrial development continents away could threaten the mountains' climate and stability. But Chinese smoke may prove more critical than a local fire.

Global warming poses serious challenges on several fronts. Forecasts suggest more rain and less snow, meaning more floods and erosion and less snowpack to conserve water until the summer. Droughts may be longer and temperatures hotter. This in turn will stress vegetation and may contribute to more insect infestation, disease, and catastrophic forest fire. Glaciers are expected to recede, lowering summer river flows and threatening fish populations. Mountain meadows may decline, as a smaller snowpack and longer growing season allows the tree line to move higher. Species may move north and uphill, displacing what we see today. One of those invading species may be people, our new neighbors migrating to a Pacific Northwest that becomes a cool, wet refuge for a storm-battered planet.

At stake is not just the beauty we're accustomed to but the resiliency of the mountain ecosystem. The forest that recolonized these mountains after the Ice Age has developed a complex weave of life in which what happens in the soil, on the ground, and in the tree canopy all affect and nourish each other. The mountains won't disappear. But the mountains as we know them may.

Washington State's population of nearly 7 million today is projected to reach 8.8 million by 2040. British Columbia is projected to grow from 4.7 million to more than 6 million in the same period. It is not difficult to imagine a doubling of the population living around the peaks sometime in the second half of this century. Generations to come will have to think more carefully about what the North Cascades mean to an ever more-urbanized population and about how to manage all the people who want to use them.

Mitch Friedman, executive director of Conservation Northwest, compares the North Cascades to an island in a highly developed Pacific Northwest that serves as "Noah's Ark" of native species. "More robust populations will have more climate resilience," he says.

The ark is already functioning. At this writing, it is encouraging that the earlier loss of species appears to be reversing and some are coming back. The bald eagle, wolf, grizzly bear, wolverine, and fisher are examples of species either recolonizing on their own, from Canada, or that appear likely to flourish if reintroduced.

These charismatic critters are just the tip of the iceberg, however. What's exciting about the North Cascades is how little we still know about it: how its ecosystems function, what it needs for forest and meadow health, and the genetic treasures

A black-tailed deer stands alone in an old–growth forest along Cascade River Road, Mount Baker–Snoqualmie National Forest.

its species represent. Because the mountains go from wet to dry, and from low to high, they represent belts of ecosystem that might thrive or vanish under future changes.

The wilderness also becomes a storehouse of organisms that might prove valuable in rehabilitating regions hit hard by warming or development. Call it ark or piggy bank, the range is an insurance policy for the future.

Scientists say ecosystems work best when they are large and interconnected so that organisms can move, mate, and adapt to change. New wildlife bridges being built over and under an expanded Interstate 90 will help link the North Cascades to the southern ecosystems around Mounts Rainier, Adams, and Saint Helens. From there, a protected Chehalis River valley could provide a link to another eco-island, the Olympic Peninsula and Olympic National Park.

To the north, Canadians are working to sustain migratory corridors between their portion of the North Cascades and the Coast Mountains ecosystems to the northwest. To the east, a proposal for a national park in British Columbia would sustain wild corridors that would allow biological communication from the North Cascades and Pasayten mountains to the Columbia Highlands and Kootenay mountains.

Ultimately, the North Cascades could be relinked to the American and Canadian Rockies as they were before settlement. Picture an international Pacific Northwest made up of a web of ecosystem islands that provide biologic resilience in a warming world. On such a map, the North Cascades are smack in the center.

The mountains are not just a series of ecosystems, of course. They mirror human needs and values. They have evolved from a commodity storehouse of minerals and timber to psychological sanctuary and recreational playground. In an increasingly frenetic world, they are the place our grandchildren will go for challenge, contemplation, and fun. Some will dangle from rock walls, some will prowl in RVs, some will hunt deer and others butterflies, some will study and some will seek to unclutter the mind, but the social and political importance of the North Cascades is certain to grow.

Different strategies may emerge.

One idea is to expand North Cascades National Park itself, providing more unity in management of the ecosystem. This might range from the modest—incorporating existing recreation areas and annexing adjacent valleys—to the grand. "If Mount Baker were included, North Cascades National Park would be an iconic park like Yellowstone, Yosemite, the Grand Canyon, and Denali," says the National Park Service's Chip Jenkins. He's not advocating such inclusion but simply noting how we still fragment these mountains in our management of them.

An alternative to expansion, although not necessarily contradictory, is to identify the North Cascades not by the park boundaries but by the broader ecological ones, looking at the 2.7 million acres of protected land as a holistic opportunity for research, recreation, and ecosystem management. Government agencies and local communities can work ever more closely together to reinforce the health and utility of the mountains.

A related notion is to expand the twentieth-century idea of mountain refuges to a much more integrated approach that extends into the lowlands, to rivers and bottomlands, following the ecology the way elk move up and down the slopes. In this approach, salmon become a thread connecting saltwater protection to the health of mountain river valleys, and glaciers and lakes are cherished for their watering of the lower world. We

A park ranger shares stories of ecosystems, geology, and natural and cultural history of the region with North Cascades Institute's Mountain School students.

begin to look at the landscape as an integrated whole, as nature does. Riparian corridors along streams become more strands of the web extending from the mountains. Instead of just saving the glorious peaks, we would be interested in linking ecosystems from saltwater to glacier.

Conservation Northwest's Friedman suggests "giving the animals a break" by putting less emphasis on backcountry adventure and more on recreational development in the foothills. New generations of trail runners and bicyclists are using the backcountry differently than their parents. Could opportunities in the Chuckanuts or similar hills remove pressure on high-mountain meadows and lessen carbon emissions from hikers seeking the freedom of the hills?

Now that logging and mining have been globalized and regional markets have shrunk, do the North Cascades provide sufficient economic opportunity for mountain communities? While Suncadia, Leavenworth, Winthrop, and Chelan are examples of what is possible, could there be strategic placement of interpretive centers, campgrounds, outdoor schools, and easily negotiable paths that bring more diversity among visitors? What kinds of mountain experience make sense for racial minorities, the elderly, the disabled, urbanites, and the rural? Can the North Cascades be not just an ecological connector, but a social one? Do existing opportunities reflect the makeup of twenty-first-century America?

Another question is whether it makes sense to have policies switch at the forty-ninth parallel. Are there more opportunities for cooperation between Canada and the United States? One policy difference is that Canada provides auto access to the upper end of Ross Lake while the American North Cascades Highway is connected to the lower lake only by a short trail. The United States tends to emphasize the wilderness aspect of the North Cascades, while the Canadians—with huge expanses of wilderness to the north—have put more recreational development on the border. Since the reservoir crosses the international line, is the present management cooperation adequate?

Are teaching institutions and organizations, such as the Environmental Learning Center on Diablo Lake and The Mountaineers, examples of the future utility of these peaks? Will the North Cascades become temple, monastery, or church where we come to understand our own civilization and its problems?

Each summer the North Cascades Institute takes high school students on a two-week adventure into the mountains, including a hike up Desolation Peak where Jack Kerouac once sojourned. I met some in Devils Canyon, a heavenly grotto where Ross Lake winds back into Devils Creek gorge. The sun, dancing on the clear water, cast undulating light waves on the surrounding cliffs and their hanging gardens of fern and trees.

"The mountains stretched out like a map," Sherwin Shabder of Olympia told me, describing the view from Desolation that he'd risen at 5:00 a.m. to climb. "The mountains looked like they could fit in your pocket."

"You can listen to yourself," said Cristina Gonzalez of Burlington. "I learned who I am as a person."

Jeanette Johnson of Olympia had jotted down her impressions: "The big hard sun is up there to beat down. The big green reaches toward the sky. The good earth breathes."

What these students found was life changing. "I want to help the environment so people can experience what I've experienced," said Richard Perkins of Kelso.

"One person really can change the world," said Jenny Wall of Walla Walla.

Then they went back ashore and slipped into the forest, absorbed into the mountains once again.

In the last two hundred years—which is a blink in geologic and biological time—the North Cascades have passed from aboriginal use and habitation to a tightly defined reserve in the middle of postindustrial civilization. The mountains have gone from being traversed by a few hundred hunter-gatherers to being surrounded by seven million urbanites. They have evolved from an Eldorado for prospectors to a sanatorium for cubicle workers.

"The question is not just what's working today," says Park Service deputy regional director Jenkins, "but what happens to an ecosystem of value when it is surrounded by *fourteen* million people."

"Our goal should be to have a sustainable ecosystem next to this megalopolis," Friedman says. "It doesn't solve the world's problems, but it's cool in its own right." The North Cascades are not just an ark, he says. They're a lifeboat.

The wilderness experience always evolves. In our imagined camping spot, on our wilderness journey, the thunder mutes and a storm passes. The sky burns with stars. The warmth of a campfire, a comfort since prehistoric times, is prohibited in the high backcountry. There are simply too many hikers, too little wood, and too high a risk of setting off a burn. So we watch the night sky as the animals do, the cosmos wheeling in its great circle around the North Star. Far below, the lights of cities continue to spread.

Looking back on my Mount Baker climb and its rumbling avalanches, and all the experiences the mountains have granted since—mirrored lakes, precipitous trails, roaring falls, a curious marmot, hummingbirds in a seven-thousand-foot-high meadow, Indian rock shelters, a wintry ski run, bighorn sheep that tolerate my presence, feasting eagles—I see the gift of grace.

The mountains talk to anyone who listens, while understanding just what they're saying can take a lifetime. They summon, I think, what Lincoln called "the better angels of our nature." They tell us we're not alone and remind us to make room for the organisms we share the planet with. They beckon us to explore.

The peaks, first. And through those peaks, ourselves.

HUMAN HISTORY IN THE NORTH CASCADES

BY WILLIAM DIETRICH

What we designated "wilderness" in the North Cascades, Native Americans called home. Pioneer beliefs that Native tribes avoided the North Cascades have been overturned by archeological finds led by national park archeologist Bob Mierendorf. His teams have discovered more than 260 mountain sites with Native American use, 45 at elevations higher than four thousand feet. Use of a rock shelter next to Newhalem Creek near the North Cascades Highway, easily viewed today from an elevated boardwalk dates back to more than a thousand years ago. Fire hearths were in use at Cascade Pass an astonishing 9,600 years ago, and flint was being mined near Hozomeen Mountain that long ago. That's twice the age of the Great Pyramid of Giza in Egypt.

The test pits at Cascade Pass have striking layers of dirt, ash, and Native artifacts laid down like a layer cake. New soil has been added since the last ice age scraped the pass bare, including volcanic ash from eruptions as far away as Oregon's Mount Mazama, 7,700 years ago. This layering allows precise dating of the unearthed stone tools and fire pits. "Postholes can be like sonar into the past," the archeologist told me.

The evidence shows that Native Americans were not just hurrying over the high country, Mierendorf says. They were camping there for some time, gathering berries and hunting meat. In the long history of Native use, the climate warmed and cooled and glaciers advanced and receded, meaning the mountains may have been more accessible, with more food, in certain periods.

Historic Native attitudes toward these mountains are hard to determine. By the late nineteenth century, when scholars began anthropological inquiries, diseases introduced by Europeans had reduced Northwest Coast populations by 80 percent. When Henry Custer canoed down the upper Skagit River in 1859 to the site of today's Ross Dam, he found Indian trails on the banks decaying from disuse. Pioneers had little interest in recording the ecological knowledge of tribes, and many oral memories were lost.

We do know that Native settlements, both permanent and seasonal, occurred high along mountain rivers such as at Marblemount, Newhalem, Mazama, Leavenworth, and Index. Highly prized mountain goat wool and chert were traded with coastal tribes, and Columbia River salmon ascended into the eastern Cascades.

Mountaineer and historian Fred Beckey has estimated that the aboriginal population of the periphery of the North Cascades was probably not higher than ten thousand in pioneer times. An 1855 census listed the Skagit Tribe as having 1,300 members; the Lummi, Nooksack, and Samish 1,050; and the Snoqualmie and Snohomish 1,700. In Canada the western mountains were used by the Stó:lō Tribe, while the upper Skagit Valley was the realm of the Nlakápamux (Lower Thompson) Tribe. East of the Cascades were the Okanogan, Methow, Chelan, Entiat, Wenatchi, and Similkameen tribes. Nooksack settlements could be found along the North Fork of the Nooksack River as far upstream as Canyon Creek.

Spectacular pictographs from the Chelan Tribe may still be seen in undisclosed areas on cliffs in the Lake Chelan region. The paintings were made with red ocher, a natural form of iron oxide. The upraised arm suggests a hunter driving the animals off a cliff, with the suggestion of a cliff edge created by the natural crack in the rock. The zoomorphic figures appear to be mountain goats, rare in pictographs.

This pictograph is similar in pigmentation and design elements to others that cover the area between northcentral Washington and adjacent southern British Columbia. This rock art is a type of public art created to appeal to spiritual powers for assistance with spirit questing and the acquisition of hunting prowess.

A facsimile panel of one of the Lake Chelan pictographs, as well as examples of tools used by native people of the North Cascades, can be seen in the North Cascades Visitor Center at Newhalem.

Left: Upper Skagit tribal biologists scan the chinook salmon catch for coded-wire tags that were inserted into the fish before they were released from a hatchery as juveniles. Right: Industrial and agricultural pollution and dams that block fish migration and access to spawning habitat have resulted in declines of salmon and steelhead populations in northwest rivers. Yakama Nation Fisheries' strategies include both habitat recovery and supplementing salmon runs. If more juvenile fish survive their first year in the river, and are larger and stronger for their migration downstream to the ocean, more fish survive and return later as adults. Large constructed habitats, such as this recent ambitious project on the Entiat River, mimic the natural processes of large trees from mature forests falling into the river. This encourages natural processes to take over and rebuild the deep, cool pools, forest cover, and woody debris ideal for naturally spawned steelhead and salmon.

The mountains were a grocery store. Upper Skagit Indians fished with nets, weirs, spears, and hooks. Natives hunted deer, elk, bear, beaver, and goat and ate at least eighteen kinds of berry and seven different roots. They used snowshoes, knapped flint, set fires, and maintained trails. Mierendorf has found arrow and spearheads, stone tools, animal bone, and hearth ashes.

The archeological discoveries are not just of academic importance. When the North Cascades were designated wilderness and park, they were assumed to be unchanged by human activities. We now know that they were never "untrammeled," which is how federal law defined wilderness, but in fact were hunted, fished, traversed, and harvested. Mierendorf believes this could help provide realism and flexibility in mountain management. "There are few places on the globe humans haven't messed with," he says. "Enthusiasts need to prove wilderness was always there to justify more wilderness today, but humans have been in the North Cascades a very long time."

Acknowledging this, he argues, encourages less rigidity and more common sense in what to allow or ban from wilderness

Native Americans used trails across the mountains that were different from the passes used by automobiles today. Lake Chelan was an obvious artery. Stehekin means "the way through," and the commonest cross-mountain route consisted of a canoe trip up Lake Chelan, an ascent of the Stehekin Valley to Cascade Pass, and then a descent down the Cascade River to Marblemount and the Skagit Valley. Farther south, near today's US Highway 2, a Lake Wenatchee Indian trail followed the White River west to Indian Pass and down the Sauk River. Snoqualmie Pass was also an aboriginal foot trail, but when John F. Stevens found Stevens Pass in 1890 there was no evidence of Native trails there.

areas. This doesn't mean that we should permit logging, mining, hunting, or tourism development, but rather that we understand and learn from the landscape's long coevolution with humans who were part of the ecology.

Natives can offer their own perspectives on the mountains and their management. Present-day tribes in and around the North Cascades include Canada's Stó:lō and Nlakápamux (Lower Thompson) tribes. East of the Cascades in the United States, the Chelan Tribe is part of the Confederated Tribes of the Colville Reservation. On the western side near the mountains are the Nooksack, Upper Skagit, Sauk-Suiattle, Snoqualmie, Stillaguamish, and Tulalip tribes. Somewhat further afield, the Lummi Tribe has an interest in the Nooksack drainage and the Yakama Nation is involved in conservation work in the Methow watershed within the national forest.

They have sustained fishing, hunting, gathering, worship, and wildlife management activities in the mountains and are working with archeologists and anthropologists in learning more about the past.

EARLY EXPLORERS
AND PIONEERS

BY WILLIAM DIETRICH

European encounters with the North Cascades date back to Manuel Quimper's Spanish expedition of 1790 and George Vancouver's British exploration of 1792. Both sailed the San Juan Islands and identified Mount Baker from the sea, with British third lieutenant Joseph Baker getting honors for spotting it from HMS *Discovery*. Spanish pilot Gonzalo López de Haro had charted the mountain as La Gran Montaña del Carmelo.

The first known white man to cross the range was fur trader and explorer Alexander Ross, who ascended Lake Chelan to Cascade Pass in 1814 and descended to the west side via the usual Native route. His account of the journey is vague.

Captain George McClellan (the future Civil War general) scouted the eastern slopes of the North Cascades in 1853, passing along the southern shore of Lake Chelan. This trip was enough to persuade him there was no railroad route to be had, and he did not penetrate the mountains very far.

From the west, railroad surveyor D.C. Linsley ascended the Suiattle River to Suiattle Pass in 1870 and later traveled from the foot of Lake Chelan to the mouth of the Stehekin River and up the valley to Agnes Creek. American army officers went up Lake Chelan by canoe in 1879 and crossed Cascade Pass in 1882, but the slopes on either side were daunting for a wagon road and

impractical for a railroad. John Stevens, a railroad surveyor, did not find the railroad and highway pass later named for him until 1890, and Stevens's map of railroad routes dismissed the rugged area around today's national park. The upper Skagit watershed wasn't accurately mapped until 1908.

Surveyors did plunge into the North Cascades to fix the international boundary. Marking the line in the riotous tangle of the North Cascades was a challenge, and successive American and British expeditions were launched between 1857 and 1862 to carry out this feat. The Americans marched from today's Lynden up the Whatcom Trail to the Sumas River and then east to a roller coaster of peaks. While exploring, they killed some grizzly bears, evidence that the species is endemic, historically, to the range. American surveyor Henry Custer benefitted from being guided by Chief Thiusoloc and from a map he drew of the area.

By 1861, some 161 iron pillars, pyramids of stones, and other types of markers had been set between Point Roberts, on the Salish Sea, to the Rocky Mountains. Fixing just one geographic point in the North Cascades required 166 observations of 48 pairs of stars to triangulate the position, taken over five cold nights one November.

For the next several decades, however, the North Cascades remained largely unknown. The mountains were not on the way to anything, and some held that the Skagit Gorge was haunted by Native demons known as Stetattle.

Then came gold. Albert Bacon reportedly found a twenty-three-ounce gold nugget in Ruby Creek (so named because John Sutter thought that garnets he found looked like rubies) in April of 1879, and Jack Rowley found gold in nearby Canyon Creek the same year. Imposing 9,066-foot Jack Mountain, crowned

Abandoned building close to the historic town of Nighthawk in the Similkameen Valley in Okanogan County

by the Nohokomeen Glacier, is named for Rowley. By August, sixty-two prospectors were panning for metal, eventually taking out about $100,000 of placer gold.

To get to Ruby Creek, which flows into the Skagit near what is today the lower end of Ross Lake, the prospectors began building the Goat Trail through the previously impassable Skagit Gorge. The North Cascades Highway breezes through what was then an improbable patchwork of winding catwalks, perilous bridges, and half tunnels hacked into the cliffside, just high enough for passage of a packhorse. The Goat Trail culminated in a turn called Devils Corner, a scratch in the cliff a hundred sheer feet above the raging Skagit, where the first highway tunnel is today. The power of spring floods was evident from driftwood and high-water marks thirty feet above the summer stream.

Other names inspired by the route were Jacobs Ladder, Abrahams Slide, Frightful Chasm, Perpendicular Rock, Wilsons Creep Hole, and Break Neck Peak.

Eventually more than 2,500 prospectors made their way to Ruby Creek, steamboating up the Skagit to Goodells Landing at today's Newhalem. They trudged from there, pulling pack-horses and mules over icy stretches of the Goat Trail, one miner in the lead with the reins and another hauling toward the hillside by the animal's tail. The mining camp at Ruby Creek included two thousand people, boasting shops, saloons, and at least one brothel. African American George Holmes established a cabin on Ruby Creek and lived there until he died in 1925.

Despite colder weather than today—fifteen feet of snow was routinely recorded at the mouth of the creek in winter—at least six hundred claims dotted the Ruby Creek area, and there were many others elsewhere in the North Cascades, staked as high as seven thousand feet in Boston Basin near Cascade Pass.

A second gold (and silver) rush beginning in the late 1880s and early 1890s attracted miners to valleys east of Ruby Creek at Barron, to Thunder Creek, the Cascade River area, Monte Cristo, Mount Baker, and more. Newspapers claimed that Stehekin had five thousand miners at its busiest. From 1890 to 1937, more than five thousand claims were staked in the Mount Baker Mining District alone. Mining tunnels and heaps of spoils can still be spotted in the range.

Most miners went home poor, but the Lone Jack Mine near Mount Baker reportedly produced $550,000 in the last twenty-two years of its twenty-seven year existence; the Tin Cup Mine on Mount Larabee, $1.5 million. The Sunset Mine near Index produced 1.2 million pounds of copper at its peak in 1929.

The Silver Tip vein was named for an old grizzly spotted at Hannegan Pass, a popular hiking spot today. Nearby Dead Mans Camp was named for a man who disappeared while goat hunting. His wife asked that the camp be left as it was, a kind of wilderness memorial, and so it stayed until it rotted away.

The Fourth of July Mine was the claim of Mighty Joe Morovits who gave his (misspelled) name to Morovitz Creek and Morovitz Meadow on Mount Baker. A Paul Bunyan character of prodigious strength (similar to the Iron Man of the Hoh of Olympic Peninsula fame), the hermit hauled a 2,300-pound ore crusher up Swift Creek by winching it from tree to tree, a task that took him two years. He carried one-hundred-pound packs of supplies the thirty-two miles from the general store at Birdsview, on the Skagit River, to his homestead above Baker Lake. Morovits reached Mount Baker's summit alone in 1892, led numerous climbing expeditions, and made significant geologic observations. He came out of the mountains after twenty-seven years with just $175 of prospected gold.

The one North Cascades mine to produce significant ore was Holden, west of Lake Chelan. In the first half of the twentieth century it produced 212 million pounds of copper, 40 million pounds of zinc, 2 million ounces of silver, and 600,000 ounces of gold. The mine closed in 1957 and was donated to a Lutheran group in the early 1960s, which turned it into a church retreat. Today, 120 badly polluted acres along Railroad Creek are being cleaned up in a joint project involving several government agencies and mining companies.

The influx of miners created a need for detailed maps and the US Geologic Survey, a cadre of mountain-man-tough surveyors in those days, began filling in the blank spots in 1895.

In 1898, Mrs. Lucinda J. Davis and her three children built a homestead on Cedar Bar near today's Diablo, which evolved into a hotel and guest ranch. The mountains were no good for farming, cattle, or domestic sheep, but a few colorful hermits lived in the remote valleys. Tommy Roland, a well-known character who had a cabin at the foot of Jack, was institutionalized after revealing himself to be the Prophet Elisha. John McMillan, the trapper, prospector, and homesteader who opened a trail to Ruby Creek, lived on Big Beaver Creek. Early Stehekin homesteaders included William Purple, Robert Pershall, and William Buzzard. The Buckner family began wintering over in the Stehekin Valley in 1915 and formed the nucleus of a community that clung to the valley with barnacle-like adherence.

By the early twentieth century, pioneer communities were established in virtually all the river valleys leading into the North Cascades and most remain today, with economies that combine tourism, logging, and maintenance of dams, highways, and powerlines. Meanwhile, harsh weather and a lack of economic opportunity and education caused homesteads and miner cabins to largely disappear from what would become national park and wilderness.

Above: The men and accommodations both were rugged at the mining camp of Barron, near Harts Pass and the crest of the North Cascades in Okanogan County. Below: Devils Corner and the Goat Trail above the Skagit River in the 1890s. Devils Corner was one of the tightest trail sections through the Skagit River Gorge, east of today's Newhalem. The North Cascades Highway was blasted into the mountainside above this spot, about where a tunnel is now.

NORTH CASCADES
TIMELINE

9,600 BP Aboriginal habitation dates back to at least this time.

1790 Mount Baker is included on a map by Spanish ship pilot Gonzalo López de Haro.

1792 Mount Baker is named for British lieutenant Joseph Baker on Captain George Vancouver's ship *Discovery*.

1850 Approximate end of Little Ice Age.

1853 Future Civil War general George McClellan scouts the eastern slopes but fails to find key passes.

1857 Expeditions begin to survey and mark the international border through the North Cascades.

1868 A wagon road is established over Snoqualmie Pass.

1868 First ascent of Mount Baker by Edmund Coleman.

1872 Yellowstone becomes the nation's first national park.

1879 Gold is found at Ruby Creek, setting off a series of gold rushes.

1888 First settler homesteads at Stehekin.

1889 First steamer is launched on Lake Chelan.

1890 Railroad surveyor John Stevens finds Stevens Pass.

1891 First road over Blewett Pass is completed.

1893 The mining town of Monte Cristo is founded.

1893 The first railroad across Stevens Pass is completed.

1893 First proposals for a North Cascades Highway. The suggested routes based on existing mapping prove impractical.

1897 The federal government creates 3.6 million acres of "forest reserve" in Washington, including much of the North Cascades.

1897 First ascent of Glacier Peak by Thomas Gerdine and others.

1899 Mount Rainier National Park is established.

1900 The first Cascade railroad tunnel is completed at Stevens Pass.

1903 Lake Chelan Dam is completed after two earlier dams wash out.

1904 First public North Cascades trail is established, along Swift Creek near Mount Baker.

1905 The federal forest reserves become "national forests" under a new agency, the Forest Service.

1905 First automobile crossing of Snoqualmie Pass.

1907 Engineers begin to survey the Skagit Canyon for hydropower.

1909 First railroad through Snoqualmie Pass is completed.

1910 Avalanche kills ninety-six railroad passengers and crew at Stevens Pass.

1911 First Mount Baker Marathon, a race from Bellingham to the summit is held.

1916 National Park Service is created.

1916 Bills are introduced in Congress to make Mount Baker a national park. They fail.

1919 Construction of the first Gorge Dam on the Skagit River begins.

1926 Big Beaver Creek and Bacon Creek fires make firefighting a Forest Service priority in the North Cascades. More than six hundred fire lookouts are built in Washington in the coming years.

1926 The Mount Baker Park Division of the Mount Baker National Forest (later known as the Mount Baker Recreation Area) is established.

1927 Mount Baker Lodge is built, with one hundred rooms.

1930 Diablo Dam is completed.

1931 Mount Baker Lodge burns, not replaced because of the Depression.

1931 Glacier Peak–Cascade Recreation Unit is established.

1931 Whatcom Primitive Area is established.

1932 Canada's Crowsnest Highway (Highway 3) is established.

1934 First cabins built at what will become British Columbia's Cathedral Lakes Lodge.

1935 North Cascade Primitive Area is established.

1936 Mountain Loop Highway construction begins between Granite Falls and Darrington.

1937 First rope tow at Mount Baker Ski Area begins operation.

1937 First rope tows at Snoqualmie Pass and Stevens Pass begin operation.

1937 Ice Peaks National Park is proposed. The idea is defeated.

1938 Olympic National Park is established.

1938 Large-scale mining begins at Holden, near Lake Chelan.

1941 Manning Provincial Park is established.

1949 Ross Dam is completed.

1951 Stevens Pass Highway opens.

1952 Poet Gary Snyder sojourns as a fire lookout on Crater Mountain.

1952 First rope tow at Manning Provincial Park begins operation.

1956 Blewett Pass road is rerouted through Swauk Pass, but locals get pass name changed back to Blewett in 1992.

1957 Holden Mine shuts down.

1960 Glacier Peak Wilderness is established.

1964 Congress passes the Wilderness Act. Glacier Peak Wilderness is confirmed under the new law.

1966 Mission Ridge Ski Area opens.

1967 Kennecott Copper proposes an open-pit copper mine at Glacier Peak.

1968 The Wild and Scenic Rivers Act.

1968 Pasayten Wilderness is established.

1968 North Cascades National Park is established.

1968 Cathedral Provincial Park is established.

1968 Seattle City Light begins to move ahead on plans to raise Ross Dam.

1972 North Cascades Highway opens.

1973 Skagit Valley Provincial Recreation Area is created. (Redesignated as a Provincial Park in 1997.)

1976 Alpine Lakes Wilderness is established.

1978 Designation of the Skagit, Sauk, North Fork Sauk, Suiattle, and Cascade Rivers as Wild and Scenic.

1984 Boulder River, Mount Baker, Lake Chelan–Sawtooth, Noisy-Diobsud, and Henry M. Jackson wilderness areas are established.

1984 In an 80-year treaty between the United States and Canada, Seattle City Light agrees not to raise Ross Dam.

1984 First wolves in living memory spotted on American side of the border in the North Cascades.

1988 The Washington Parks Wilderness Act which established the Steven Mather Wilderness within the North Cascades National Park complex.

1994 Northwest Forest Plan severely curtails logging in Mount Baker–Snoqualmie National Forest.

1998 First production vineyards are planted around Lake Chelan.

1999 Seattle City Light begins paying $100 million to mitigate dam environmental damage.

2001 Snowy Mountain Protected Area is established.

2008 Wild Sky Wilderness is established.

Sunrise on Liberty Bell above Washington Pass, as seen from the North Cascades Highway (State Route 20). The two summits on the left are Early Winters Spires.

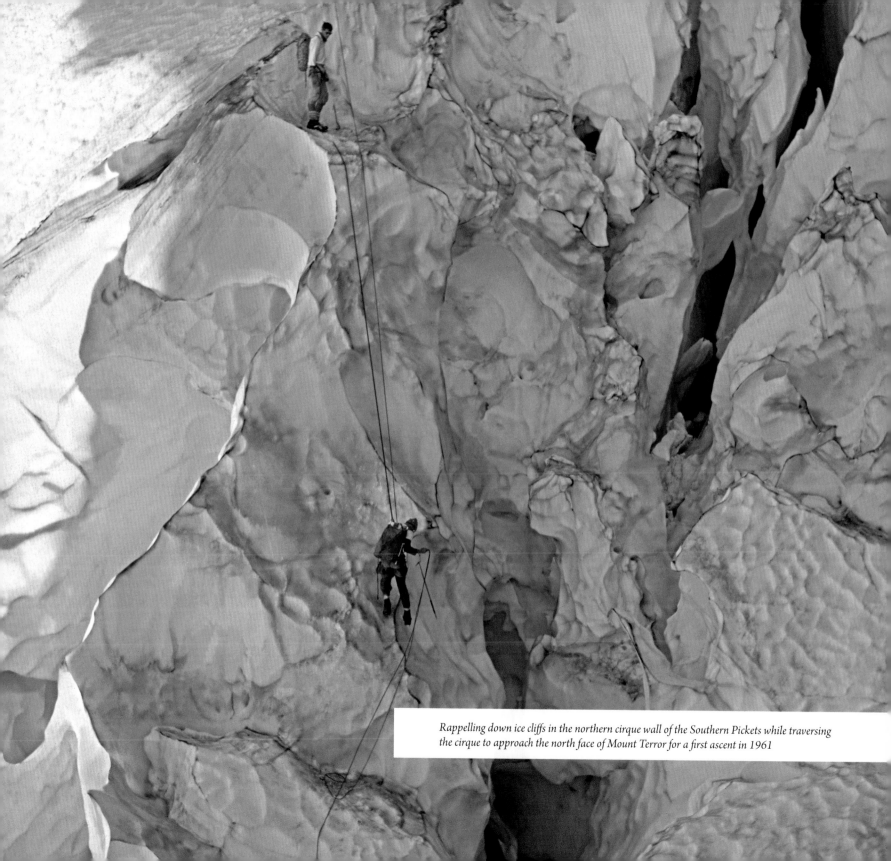

Rappelling down ice cliffs in the northern cirque wall of the Southern Pickets while traversing the cirque to approach the north face of Mount Terror for a first ascent in 1961

The trunk of a giant old-growth western red cedar, along the Baker River Trail in Mount Baker–Snoqualmie National Forest. These trees can reach more than 200 feet in height, 13 feet in diameter, and live well over 1,000 years.

PROFILES IN THE NORTH CASCADES

Humans have long calculated the worth of a given landscape based upon the exploitation of its natural resources: timber, rock, hydropower, minerals. The North Cascades, stewarded as public lands since 1897, reminds us that nature's value extends far beyond economic gains. The following profiles show just a few of the many ways in which protected wild lands reward our society: as crucibles for education, conservation, artistic and literary inspiration, scientific exploration, athletic challenge, and more. These are inestimable benefits that are seldom captured by calculator or balance sheet.

BY CHRISTIAN MARTIN

JON RIEDEL

GLACIER GEOLOGIST

What do you do if you are a young midwestern college graduate with a degree in geology and a yearning for adventure, wilderness, and outdoor work in the West? "You go to where the action is," says Jon Riedel, and for him, that meant the North Cascades.

The North Cascades' superlative features would excite any geologist: it's the most glaciated region in the Lower 48, with the most vertical relief; the bedrock floor of Lake Chelan sits more than two thousand feet below sea level; dozens of ice ages and glaciations have contorted the landscape into an infinite number of "problems" waiting to be solved. And better yet, the region had largely been ignored by geologists due to its remoteness and difficult access. Riedel found his calling and soon landed a job with North Cascades National Park as a geologist.

"The deductive approaches used in geomorphology—the study of the earth's surface—caught on with me," he explains. "The ability to read the landscape and see into the past was intoxicating."

Coming from the Midwest, Riedel found that everything in the North Cascades was different: the brush was thick and the slopes steep, making exposed rock difficult to find and study sites challenging to get to. So Riedel focused on more easily visible surficial geology features such as alluvial fans, floodplains, terraces, moraines, valleys, and of course, glaciers. With persistence

and many miles underfoot, Riedel began to understand what makes the North Cascades unique.

Because the mountains here have been uplifted rapidly and eroded intensely, volcanic rock more common to the south has been stripped away to expose metamorphic rocks brought up from great depths. In the North Cascades, it is possible to access the crystalline core that originated ten miles below the earth's surface, including Skagit gneiss, the rock that Riedel calls "the backbone of the North Cascades."

The region's glaciation history is distinct. The North Cascades were shaped by local alpine glaciers that grew from mountains down to valleys as well as by continental ice sheets moving slowly from Canada to smother the entire range in ice more than a mile thick. Shaped by multiple ice ages, "the North Cascades are a composite of millions of years of glaciations," says Riedel.

One of Riedel's most important contributions to the understanding of the North Cascades is his Glacier Monitoring Program, which he started in 1993. The study records seasonal surface accumulation of snow and the loss of snow and ice to melting—annual volume change, or mass balance—of four glaciers at different elevations with different aspects draining to different rivers. Riedel and his team visit the glaciers at least twice a year to take measurements against their melt stakes. They also

survey the total area of all glaciers in the national park every twenty years.

"Glaciers are dramatic indicators of climate change," explains Riedel. "They are sensitive to temperature because that is what determines what form of precipitation falls—snow versus rain—as well as the length and magnitude of the melt season."

For example, the 1 degree Celsius increase in temperature over the last century has melted half of the glacial area in the North Cascades. "The loss is staggering," he says. "When we look at the past twenty years, the North Cascades glaciers have shed four hundred million cubic meters of water loss. This is billions of gallons of water lost into Puget Sound, equivalent to 650,000 Olympic swimming pools, or forty-five years of water supply for Skagit County, or one month of continuous flow of the Skagit River, ten billion gallons per day for thirty days."

This rapid loss of North Cascades glaciers affects local agriculture, municipal water supplies, industry, hydropower that lights up Seattle, and of course, a broad spectrum of species, from the little-understood ice worms that live on the glaciers to pikas in the alpine zone to the endangered salmon downstream.

"Our biggest glacier is Boston Glacier, at seven square kilometers," Riedel says. "Compared to the glaciers of the north, that's nothing, but our glaciers are important ecologically because they provide water in dry summers, buffering capacity, water insurance. The Skagit is the only river in the Northwest with five native salmon, and that's because of glaciers. They are a source of water and also habitat for ice worms that provide food for other species like rosy finches.

"Climate change is not something projected to happen, it is happening now. Everything is tied to climate and everything is in a state of flux right now. Glaciers are a prime indicator of this."

Then and now: the Roosevelt Coleman Glacier, Glacier Creek

FRED BECKEY
MOUNTAINEER AND AUTHOR

Perhaps no living human is more associated with the untamed allure of the North Cascades—a blend of fear, awe, agony, and ecstasy—than mountaineer Fred Beckey.

In the celebratory, life-spanning book *Fred Beckey's 100 Favorite North American Climbs*, his friends and climbing partners from the last seven decades lavish Beckey with accolades: "The most prolific mountaineer of the last 100 years," "the undisputed sovereign of American dirtbag climbers," and "grandfather of the road trip." These claims would be unbearable were they not actually true.

Beckey immigrated to Seattle from Germany with his family in 1925 and, with the Boy Scouts and local mountaineering clubs, began climbing the mountains visible from the city. He ascended Boulder Peak in the Olympic Mountains by himself at age thirteen—beginning his life's trajectory spent climbing remote rock—and later achieved the summit of Mount Olympus with his troop.

Beckey began exploring the North Cascades next, making first ascents up Mount Despair in 1939 and Forbidden Peak in 1940—rugged mountains deemed unclimbable by the local mountaineering club. Over the ensuing summers, he pioneered routes up dozens more Cascades peaks, sometimes with his brother Helmy in tow. Staring out across the sea of peaks, Beckey recounts feeling "a kinship with the noble almost unbelievable peaks and tumbling glaciers."

In 1942, the brothers made their way toward Mount Waddington in British Columbia's Coast Mountains, a dark, sulking massif cloaked in glaciers and surrounded by miles of impenetrable coastal rain forest. After weeks of rain, snow, rockfall, and avalanches, the two teenagers achieved the summit, only the second humans to stand atop the peak, and the second up the foreboding south face approach.

The accomplishment shocked the mountaineering community, left to marvel that two unknown, untrained teenagers had not only the skills and mettle but also the audacity to attempt such a feat. While not exactly antagonistic, Beckey's unorthodox style of climbing razzed the formal establishment: it was quick, improvisational, in small groups, and used nontraditional techniques and motley gear.

"I discovered that climbing required making meaningful decisions, practicing the facets of strategy, and a commitment difficult to equal in daily life," he wrote. "There was a freedom from constraints, and an intensity and happiness after a safe return."

His list of mountaineering accomplishments grew: in the summer of 1954 he climbed Mounts McKinley, Hunter, and Deborah in Alaska, a feat referred to as his Triple Crown of

First Ascents. Friends rarely knew where in the world Fred was until he stormed in to town fired up for his next secret mission in the mountains.

While the ensuing decades would find Beckey asserting his prowess on rock from the Alaska Range to the Tetons, the Sierra Nevada to the desert Southwest, he kept circling back to the endless new challenges in the North Cascades. He has lived an authentic life of adventure, hardiness, and spontaneity that thousands of mountaineers emulate today.

"Fred has done more first ascents than any other human has, or ever will," remarks Yvon Chouinard, one of Beckey's early climbing partners who went on to found the Patagonia clothing company. "He is the essence of climbing. He's never done it for money or for fame. Fred climbs for the joy of it."

Beckey's lasting imprint on the North Cascades is assured. He has named peaks in the range, written climbing guides (the *Cascade Alpine Guides*) that are widely considered the bibles of Cascades mountaineering, published an exhaustively researched tome on early exploration of the American Alps (*Challenge of the North Cascades*), and done more first ascents than he, or anyone else, can track.

Next time you're in the North Cascades, look up. What might at first appear to be a mountain goat may be Beckey, continuing his life-long love affair with these mountains.

Don Gordon belaying Fred Beckey on the first ascent of the direct east ridge of Forbidden Peak in the North Cascade mountains (May 25, 1958)

THE MOUNTAINEERS teen adventure program provides year-round opportunities for young adults to experience the outdoors. During the school year, youth ages 14–18 from around western Washington learn technical skills, independence, and leadership in the outdoors through hiking, paddling, skiing, rock climbing, and mountaineering. With time spent in the mountains, they form a tight-knit supportive community—something that is hard to come by in a typical high school environment. Over four years, participants learn from their peers, gain a clearer understanding of their own interests, and learn to teach others.

Here, participants enjoy climbing and learning about building and cleaning rock anchors at Unibolter Rock in Mazama during a week-long summer trip to the North Cascades. Programs that teach skills and encourage people to get outside to enjoy muscle-powered recreation from hiking and climbing to snowshoeing and sailing are supported by an extensive network of volunteers among the 10,000 members of The Mountaineers, an organization founded in 1906.

MOLLY HASHIMOTO
CONSERVATION ARTIST

When Molly Hashimoto began seeing the North Cascades in nighttime reveries, she knew that she would need to explore them artistically. "Sometimes I am so taken with a place that I dream about it," she explains. "When that happens, I feel compelled to try to paint it, often many different times and many different ways. In the North Cascades, I love the cool palette of blues and greens in the conifers and water, snow and sharp peaks, mists and clouds."

As a child in Denver, Hashimoto loved playing outdoors, as well as making art when the weather kept her inside. She cartooned, painted, and carved woodblocks, inspired by a high school teacher who taught her that "art wasn't just pretty pictures, but also about expressing ideas, that you could have a serious purpose as an artist."

She moved to Seattle in the 1970s, beckoned by the mountains and sea, and found her creative calling in watercolors while studying at the School of Visual Concepts. "Watercolor became my favorite medium because it is inexpensive and I can paint many different subjects, almost as fast as they occur," she says. "It is the best plein air medium and seems so appropriate for the misty, watery mountain landscapes of western Washington."

The North Cascades have inspired her work for three decades, serving as both subject and studio. The cool climate is perfect for her chosen medium—"the watercolors stay wet longer and give you plenty of time to work"—and there is no end to inspiring locations from which to paint.

"My favorite place is at Diablo Lake, where you can look up over a mile to the summit of Pyramid Peak," Hashimoto says. "I am thrilled by the drama of that sheer drop and the perfect sculpted form of the peak. I am in awe of the rich cinnamon-colored bark of the ancient trees along the Skagit River near Newhalem. I delight in heading up to the higher elevations in summer, enjoying the colors of the Golden Horn Batholith's granite, the noble Engelmann spruce trees, and in autumn, the unbelievable gold of the larches."

In her paintings, Hashimoto often focuses in on the details that enliven the North Cascades: a woodpecker, loon, or owl, wildflowers in bloom, a grove of aspen trees. Her work is representational and unembellished, allowing her subjects to speak for themselves through graceful lines, subtle coloring, and ecologically appropriate settings that reveal hints of the natural history of the species pictured.

"It's really important to me to learn as much as I can about trees and flowers and birds, to know their names and habits," she remarks, "because I believe it helps me to be a better artist."

Hashimoto fits into a lineage of artists who have recognized that the value of a given landscape is not limited to what we can take from it—that the natural beauty of wild places has worth not easily tallied in a spreadsheet—and she has attempted to share that appreciation with the rest of us. "Artists are able to see what is special and unique in the world," she notes, "and through their craftsmanship, they enable others to see that also."

Hashimoto's enthusiasm for painting untamed places has led her to teach outdoor art classes in the North Cascades, Yellowstone, in green pockets around Seattle, and even abroad in the hills of Italy.

"I try to give students a way to personally connect to the power and beauty of the natural world," she says. "When you study the milky glacial green of Diablo Lake, and actually mix the blues and umbers that can come close to mirroring that amazing color . . . you have to slow down quite a bit to do that. That time my students and I spend is a way of cherishing this place, and I truly hope that it results in all of us understanding that this beauty deserves our endless care."

BILL GAINES
WILDLIFE BIOLOGIST

As a wildlife biologist, Bill Gaines values high-quality data, significant statistics, and peer-reviewed results. But, after thirty years of studying carnivores in the North Cascades—including his ongoing search for the elusive grizzly bear—he has also relied on perseverance, sweat, tenacity, mosquito repellent, and sturdy hiking boots.

Born in Oregon, Gaines was introduced to the outdoors by his grandfather through camping, hiking, and hunting. His father worked for the US Forest Service in the southern Oregon Cascades alongside state wildlife biologists, and Gaines tagged along on trips into the backcountry at an early age.

"I fell in love with animals and being outside," he recalls. "I told my grandmother when I was twelve that I would be a wildlife biologist when I grew up."

His family moved to Washington's Methow Valley when Gaines was in high school and he got to know the state on his academic journey: Washington State University as an undergraduate, Central Washington University for his master's degree, and the University of Washington for his PhD. His childhood dream became a reality when he was hired by the US Forest Service to work on the North Cascades Grizzly Bear Ecosystem Evaluation Project in the mid-1980s, studying *Ursus arctos horribilis* populations.

"My initiation to wildlife biology in the North Cascades was hiking into these amazing places like the Napeequa River valley in the Glacier Peak Wilderness to map bear habitat," Gaines says.

Historical records indicate there was once a thriving population of grizzlies roaming the international ecosystem. However, trapping, hunting, and human encroachment drastically reduced their numbers. The last documented grizzly on the US side was shot in 1967 in Fisher Creek basin, the heart of the North Cascades. While grizzly bears in northern British Columbia remain healthy, the population is estimated to be only a handful. The evaluation project determined the North Cascades to have outstanding habitat for grizzlies and led to the region being designated an official recovery zone by the US Fish and Wildlife Service in 1991.

As he continued to work on grizzly bear recovery, Gaines was pleasantly surprised to encounter other Cascades carnivores: gray wolves wandering across the border from British Columbia, wolverines showing up on remote cameras. As of 2013, about a dozen wolverines have been radio-collared (for scientific studies) and four wolf packs now call the North Cascades home. These developments excited biologists around the region while also introducing new challenges.

"I went traveling to communities around the North Cascades giving talks about bear and wolves, explaining what these creatures are and what it means to recover them," Gaines explains. "When predators have been missing from an ecosystem for a long time and suddenly people have, say, wolves in their backyards, they can have strong reactions. Human understanding about these animals is so influenced by emotions: people worry about their personal safety, or threats to livestock and pets, or losing access to their favorite recreation areas. School prepared me for the scientific and technical side of wildlife biology, but it didn't prepare me for this social side. The emotional aspects knocked my socks off."

Gaines continued to search for grizzlies with his team, venturing into backcountry sites "where grizzly bears would be if they are here. To date, based on thousands of DNA samples and thousands of photos, we have not detected a grizzly bear in the North Cascades," he says. "While it was rewarding to put a pack on my back and go to work in places I love, it was also disheartening to come up empty-handed in the search."

Having spent the majority of his life in the North Cascades, Gaines has earned a firsthand understanding of its ecological complexity and contemporary conservation issues. He has intimate knowledge of many of the individual puzzle pieces of the ecosystem, how they fit together and which ones are missing.

"It's tremendous to have witnessed the rebound of wolverines and wolves in the North Cascades," he reflects. "It helps create a powerful positive vision of the future. But I worry about the grizzly. I don't think it will hang on without some human intervention. As a society, we need to decide what we're going to do for its recovery. I have a lot of optimism, mixed with concern, and think we have an amazing opportunity here."

So, what next?

"There are plenty of nooks and crannies grizzlies can hang out in that are tough for us to get to," Gaines says, smiling. "It keeps that mystique alive: Are they still out there? Maybe they are. I guess I'll just have to load up my backpack and keep looking!"

The rebound of the wolf population in the North Cascades offers biologists a chance to examine the complexities of maintaining a healthy and balanced ecosystem.

COLIN HALEY

CLIMBER

Colin Haley was born in Seattle in 1984 and grew up on nearby Mercer Island. For as far back as he can remember, he's been exploring the Cascades, hiking and skiing, always looking upward, drawn to the summits of the high peaks.

At the age of twelve, Haley ascended the West Ridge of Forbidden Peak in the North Cascades—named one of the "Fifty Classic Climbs of North America"—with his father and older brother. It was the beginning of a new life.

"I had climbed Mount Hood the year before," he remembers, "but Forbidden was my first technical climb. It had all the elements that make alpine climbing such a memorable pursuit: ascending a steep ridge that scared the crap out of me, rappeling the last several pitches down in the dark, getting back to camp completely exhausted. It was a taste of the physical and mental hardships that climbing mountains often puts you through and from then on, I was hooked. That's all I wanted to do with my life."

Alpine climbing became "by far the overriding focus" of Haley's life, and once he got his driver's license at age sixteen, he was in the mountains every chance he could get. Between the ages of sixteen and twenty, he figures he logged more days in the American Alps than any other climber.

"Everything I learned," he says, "I learned in the North Cascades."

It was one of the best classrooms a young, hungry climber could hope for.

"The North Cascades are the only range in the Lower 48 states with legitimate alpine terrain, besides the volcanoes to the south and a tiny bit in the Tetons," Haley explains. "People who don't climb think elevation is what's important in mountaineering, like the Colorado Rockies and Sierras with their summits of 13,000 to 14,000 feet. But they are snowless, iceless, grassy mountains. For developing mountaineering skills—navigating icefalls, crevasse rescue, traversing permanent north-facing snowfields or glaciers—the North Cascades are by far the most real mountains we have."

Unpredictable weather and a hardy climate contribute to making the range a proving ground for mountaineers. The North Cascades get pummeled with tons of precipitation from the Pacific Ocean, and it's usually cold enough to fall as snow instead of rain in the winter. Mount Baker set a world record for the most snowfall ever recorded in a single season: 1,140 inches at the ski area in 1998–99.

"Alpine climbing in the North Cascades in winter is about as hard-core as climbing gets anywhere in the world," Haley says. "These mountains are already a pretty rugged range in the summer, but in the winter they are five times more serious:

Colin Haley nearing the summit of Inspiration Peak on the first winter ascent, February 2003

access is more difficult, approaches more arduous, conditions more extreme. And snowfall amounts are often very, very big."

Because of the region's unique combination of terrain and climate, the Pacific Northwest has produced many of the most skilled American climbers, such as Tom Hornbein and Steve House. But according to Haley, one legend stands above all the rest.

"Fred Beckey is without a doubt the most accomplished climber ever to come out of North America, among the best alpinists in the world," Haley says. "His legacy of climbing, with all of his first ascents, is completely unparalleled."

Beckey, ninety-one years old and still climbing, has been a lifelong hero of Haley's, "a tangible inspiration because I grew up in the same city and learned to climb on the same peaks as him."

Like Beckey, Haley has used his time and training in the North Cascades to prepare himself for extreme expeditions in Alaska and British Columbia, as well as climbs farther afield in the Karakorum, Himalaya, and Alps. He says he's currently "obsessed" with Patagonia in southern Argentina and dreaming of new routes and traverses to explore.

"My views on nature have evolved with spending lots of time out in it," he reflects. "There is less of a separation in my mind between the human world and natural world. Friends of mine who lead the 'normal life' view the city as life, and there's this other thing out there called wilderness. I don't feel that division. I feel more immersed in nature and view ourselves as just another species who happens to have built a whole bunch of infrastructure."

"I'm glad there are places like the North Cascades," Haley says, "where we can go and climb spectacular, rugged mountains in 100 percent wilderness environments."

ANA MARIA SPAGNA

WRITER, TRAIL WORKER, STEHEKIN RESIDENT

Like many people who choose to live in the North Cascades, Ana Maria Spagna has patched together jobs, passions, and pursuits that inform and inspire each other. Through perseverance and pluck, she has created a life *and* livelihood in one of the more remote communities in America: Stehekin, a village of fewer than one hundred year-round residents that is accessible only by float plane, a three-hour boat ride, or a long hike over the mountains.

Spagna grew up in Riverside, California, but a camping trip to Oregon as a teenager connected her with the natural world of the Pacific Northwest. "I loved the green forests and the blue sky and even the rain," she remembers, "and I swore that if I ever made it back, I'd never leave."

After graduating from college, she spent a summer volunteering with the Student Conservation Association in Canyonlands National Park, which led her to apply for jobs in other parks around the West. She landed in Stehekin in 1990 at age twenty-two to work for the North Cascades National Park.

"I had never been there, didn't know you had to take a boat to get there," she admits. "I arrived and saw those mountains and was completely *wowed*!"

The community of Stehekin sits at the northwest end of Lake Chelan, a fifty-five-mile-long fjord-like lake carved by glaciers, the third-deepest lake in the country. The village is surrounded by steep mountains rising seven thousand feet above the valley floor. There are no shopping malls or Starbucks, though the internet and a few phones connect inhabitants to the outside world. Cabins are scattered for nine miles up the valley along the meandering Stehekin River. Summertime temperatures can be upward of 100 degrees Fahrenheit, while winters bring long periods of snow and subfreezing temperatures. It is a place for people who like solitude and living close to nature.

Spagna was first assigned a desk job, but she spent every weekend exploring the mountains, eventually joining a trail crew. The transitory nature of trail work had her stationed in Marblemount for a couple of years and then out of Darrington, working in the Glacier Peak Wilderness, for a few more.

She cleared trails with chainsaw, brush whips, and loppers, maintained bridges, worked on tread with a pulaski, and cleared rockslides with explosives. She would often camp in the woods for eight days at a time, putting in ten-hour days with a crew of four or five people, mostly men.

"It was empowering to learn to do the kind of work that would usually be men's work," she recalls. "Learning to use a chainsaw in particular was a challenge, but I gained confidence and endurance. I love the kind of work where you can *see* what you accomplished at the end of the day."

All the while, Spagna was writing about her unfolding life in her journal and turning her experiences into essays. She published pieces in *Orion*, *Utne Reader*, *Backpacker*, *Oregon Quarterly*, and *High Country News* about the North Cascades, trail work, and the joys and challenges of living in a remote community.

"Stehekin is a place where you see people interacting with wild country on an everyday basis," she explains. "It's really shaped how I see the world and inspired my writing. I'm very leery of anything that separates nature from the human experience. The more we can see them as integrated experiences, the better our world will be."

Her essays—displaying a keen eye for natural detail, a wry sense of humor, humility, and a generous, heartfelt style of storytelling—have been collected in the award-winning books *Now Go Home* and *Potluck*.

"Any of us doing any work, but especially writers, need some solitude, a quiet place," Spagna reflects. "There's something about a place that is left alone like the North Cascades that gives you the grounding to tell stories."

Stehekin is a remote community nestled in the northwest end of Lake Chelan, with no road access.

POLLY DYER
ENVIRONMENTAL ACTIVIST

In the North Cascades, a mosaic of public lands—national, state, and provincial parks, national forests, wilderness and recreation areas—protects many of the region's most beloved areas. It's easy to take their stewardship for granted—few today would argue against preserving natural treasures like Mount Baker, the Picket Range, Cascade Pass, and Suiattle River—but in truth, Washingtonians owe a great deal of gratitude to early visionaries like Polly Dyer.

Without Dyer and her ilk, imagine what might have been: Clear-cuts in the Stehekin Valley. A half-mile-wide open-pit copper mine in the shadow of Glacier Peak. The ancient cedars of the Little Beaver Valley drowned underwater. And elsewhere in the state, a ski area, tramway, and golf course on Mount Rainier; the Hoh River valley excised from Olympic National Park and sold for timber. Instead of the most primitive stretch of coastline in the Lower 48, a scenic highway running along the beaches from La Push to Shi Shi.

Dyer's six decades of writing letters, organizing volunteers, attending meetings, serving on committees, and lobbying legislators in both Washingtons have helped keep some of our most spectacular landscapes intact. And in the era before social media, virtual meet-ups, and online petitions, those conservation efforts required a lot of legwork, fundraising, face-to-face negotiations, and pots of coffee.

Born in Honolulu in 1920, Pauline Dyer saw a wide swath of America as her father moved around the country following Coast Guard postings: Seattle, New York City, Connecticut, Philadelphia, Baltimore, Florida, and finally, Alaska. Summers at Girl Scout camp introduced her to the natural world, but the raw wilderness of Alaska provided what she later called "the basis for my whole life since."

She met her husband, John, on the trail, and together they explored coastal areas like Glacier Bay in a sixteen-foot skiff, reading John Muir to pass the time. They moved to Berkeley, hiking the Sierra Nevada and becoming active in the Sierra Club, before finally settling down in the Seattle area in 1950, where the Cascades to the east and Olympics to the west fueled their passion for hiking, climbing, and conservation. Polly joined The Mountaineers and chaired the club's Conservation Committee; established the Pacific Northwest Chapter of the Sierra Club, the first chapter outside of California; helped lead the Olympic Park Associates; and cofounded the North Cascades Conservation Council.

Preserving wild places has been Dyer's undying passion. "It

is a priceless asset which all the dollars man can accumulate will not buy back," she testified before the US Senate, in support of what would become the Wilderness Act of 1964. With fellow conservationist Howard Zahniser, she is credited with the elegant definition of wilderness enshrined in that legislation: "an area where the earth and its community of life are untrammeled by man, where man himself is a visitor who does not remain."

Discussing her innate love of wilderness, Dyer exclaims that nature brought her "almost unbounded joy. I wanted to stretch out my arms and bring it all up close to me. I felt that it was literally a part of me."

As environmental conservation slowly took hold in the national consciousness in the 1960s, all eyes looked toward the North Cascades. The Sierra Club, Wilderness Society, The Mountaineers, and countless local groups were determined to win permanent protection for the "American Alps." The North Cascades Conservation Council had been formed in 1957 by Dyer, Phil Zalesky (a Seattle high school teacher), Patrick Goldsworthy (a University of Washington biochemist, shown in photo, above left, with Dyer), and others to push the effort forward, and their goal took years of political maneuvering, pamphleteering, petitioning, and letters to the editor. Their most canny strategy may have been leading VIPs and common citizens on hikes to see for themselves what made these mountains, valleys, and forests unlike any others in America.

President Lyndon Johnson signed the North Cascades Act in 1968, creating North Cascades National Park, Ross Lake National Recreation Area, Lake Chelan National Recreation Area, and nearly one million acres of wilderness in the neighboring Glacier Peak and Pasayten highlands.

Fall leaves along the Twisp River Trail in Lake Chelan–Sawtooth Wilderness

"Dyer's drive has been to protect wilderness areas, preserving them as places where the force of nature—rather than the will of human beings—prevails," historian Paula Becker writes. "Banding with others who fervently believe protecting wilderness areas matters, and steadily recruiting new supporters for the conservation movement, has been her life's work."

LIBBY MILLS
NATURALIST, ARTIST, TEACHER

Libby Mills's favorite bird to watch is the American dipper, but it is the American bald eagle that she has spent much of her adult life studying in the North Cascades. And when you study eagles on a river, you soon learn about salmon, for the two iconic Northwest species are intrinsically intertwined.

"I worked twenty-four winters on the upper Skagit River, studying the eagles and salmon, the river and forest and all those interactions," Mills explains. "This is something everyone in the Northwest should know about to be ecologically literate."

Growing up in Seattle, Mills spent most weekends exploring the outdoors on family day-trips to Green Lake or Puget Sound beaches and campouts farther afield in the Cascades and Olympics. "I learned to associate campfires with good things happening in wild places," she reminisces.

Mills's parents were naturalists who led her to pick huckleberries, explore tide pools, love wildflowers, and use a field guide. "I'd always come home muddy and never was in any trouble for it," she recalls. A curiosity for nature had long been in the family tree: Henrietta Mills, Libby's great-aunt, was one of the first women to join the Young Naturalists' Society at the University of Washington in the early 1900s.

When Mills studied at Evergreen State College, she designed a course of study she named Wilderness Philosophy Past and Present. Mills always wanted to work outdoors and spent four summers as a backcountry ranger in Mount Rainier National Park and five more in Alaska as a naturalist in Katmai and Denali national parks.

"By the time words like 'ecology' were in the common lexicon," she says, "I was studying the land and life-forms to understand how it all fit together to form the ecological story of where I live."

Like many naturalists, Mills turns to art to record her impressions and better appreciate what she is observing. She has dozens of albums of photographs and journals full of ink and colored pencil sketches. "The acts of writing and drawing help me remember the experience, draws it deeper into my brain and enhances my knowledge of it," Mills explains. "Sometimes I feel like I can slow down time when I work in my journal."

The North Cascades have served Mills as a field laboratory, plein air art studio, classroom, and home. As she's immersed herself in the biological web of life that defines the region, Mills has been inspired to share what she's discovered, motivated in part by her conservationist leanings. "People don't learn to love a place until they have been out and had memorable experiences in it," she says. Mills regularly teaches birding classes, including winter outings to see the Skagit's eagles and salmon, as well as nature journaling and drawing.

Nature, no matter the weather, is her favorite classroom.

"When we get outside, whether an urban greenway or the middle of the North Cascades, the natural world makes it easier to learn," she explains. "The quiet of nature opens the mind to the amazing facts of science, like when you learn how fungi connect all the plants in the forest and make the world go round. If you're sitting in a classroom, that's a little much to believe, but if you're out in the forest and you see a mushroom growing near the roots of a tree, see the white fibrous mycelium in the soil, you say, *Ooohhh, that's it!*"

American bald eagles, along with salmon, are iconic examples of interconnected life cycles in the Pacific Northwest.

ADINA SCOTT
OUTDOOR LEADER AND MENTOR

How can you give back to a mountain range that has given so much to you? In Adina Scott's opinion, you pass the gift of the wild nearby on to the next generation. Scott was born in Washington, D.C. in 1979 and raised in Tacoma, Washington, by parents who were avid outdoorspeople. Family vacations were spent visiting Mount Rainier and Olympic national parks, climbing nearby Pinnacle Peak, and exploring Point Defiance Park in Tacoma.

"My parents had an interesting system for introducing my brother and me to the outdoors," she remembers. "When I was three years old, we went backpacking for three days, hiking three miles a day; at four years old, it was four days, four miles. This went on for a while. Growing up, I didn't realize it wasn't necessarily the most common thing to be tromping around in the woods."

Like many, Scott didn't fully grasp the value of her alpine birthright until she put distance between herself and her home mountains. Attending college in the Midwest, eventually earning her PhD in electrical engineering, she had to go out of her way to find untamed natural areas. The deep longing she felt for the Cascade Range signaled to her that being out in the mountains was an important part of her life.

"Returning to Washington after graduation was like coming home to a playground," she says. "I appreciated it so much more, rediscovering my love for hiking and backpacking while also finding passion for mountaineering and climbing—new ways to get to interesting places."

A mountaineer with a doctorate in electrical engineering is not as incongruous as it might seem. For Scott, the two disciplines share much in common: a need for intense focus, rigorous investigation, and creative problem-solving skills. Routefinding and decision-making on Sahalee or the Sharkfin Tower in the North Cascades, for example, required observation and problem-solving skills similar to those needed for engineering challenges. Reflecting on the many benefits that outdoor recreation and exploration provided her, Scott was motivated to share these experiences with the next generation. She began volunteering with Seattle YMCA's outdoor-leadership development mountain schools, taking middle and high school youth out on wilderness trips. She led backpacking trips to Stehekin, art outings with young girls on Ross Lake, and rock climbing classes on Mount Erie near Anacortes.

In 2012, Scott was contacted by the National Outdoor Leadership School with an offer to join Expedition Denali, a team of African-American climbers aiming to summit the highest peak in North America in order to inspire young people of color to get outside and explore America's wild places. Along with some of her teammates, she trained in the Waddington Range of British Columbia and together they summited Mount Baker.

Their attempt on Denali in 2013 was thwarted at 19,600 feet by a rare electrical storm, but they had accrued enough enthusiasm and experience to tour local schools and talk with students about opportunities in the outdoors. Scott was especially excited to connect with kids who hadn't thought of adventure recreation as something they could do. "There are misconceptions about what camping and hiking are all about, and the risks involved," she explains. "People of color not coming from an outdoorsy background can find it really intimidating. I want to make outdoor recreation more accessible." One of Scott's main goals is to motivate minorities to find their own routes to experiencing their wild backyards.

"It is very powerful taking minority youth outdoors," Scott says. "Wilderness travel forces everyone to operate outside of their comfort zones in an equalizing sort of way. Youth with no experience outside of the city are able to embrace challenges together because they are being challenged in a similar way. This is especially valuable for kids who feel like outsiders in their communities."

Back home preparing for a new job as an instrument technician at Palmer Station in Antarctica, Scott reflects on how the protected landscapes in Washington have shaped her career trajectory: "I've always loved going outside, exploring, observing how things are connected. I spent a huge amount of time as a child playing in the dirt, and being able to have that creative free-play in this amazing playground shaped my ability to ask questions about how the world works.

"I would not be on the path that I am on without these experiences," she concludes, "and I want younger people of all backgrounds to have those opportunities too."

Team decision-making on Mount Baker

SAUL WEISBERG

EDUCATOR AND CONSERVATIONIST

When Saul Weisberg and his climbing buddy Tom Fleischner created a nonprofit conservation organization in the mid-1980s, they consulted the *I Ching*. They were wondering how to make a livelihood from the things that they valued most: exploring the North Cascades, studying the region's natural history, working toward conservation of its wild beauty. The ancient Chinese oracle gave them a two-word reply: *perseverance furthers.*

"We didn't know what the hell that meant at the time," Weisberg recalls, almost thirty years into his tenure as executive director of North Cascades Institute, "but we do now: stay the course!"

Born in New York City and raised in the suburbs of Cleveland, Weisberg headed west after an unorthodox course of study at Antioch College. He followed the inspiring writings of Gary Snyder, Jack Kerouac, and Philip Whalen to Washington State in 1976 and has been here ever since. "Gray, rainy, snow-capped mountains . . . it felt like home to me," he recalls.

Weisberg got to know his adopted place by working long hours close to the land as a fisherman, fire lookout, fish hatchery technician, oyster farmer, and wildlands firefighter. In 1979, he got a summer job as a backcountry ranger for North Cascades National Park while pursuing a graduate degree in biology at Western Washington University.

"I remember being out in the mountains ten days at a time," Weisberg says, "moving by 5:00 a.m. on patrol in deep dark forest, long climbs up ridges and across glaciers, extended stretches spent above the trees . . . and then coming back to my cabin in Marblemount, staying up late at night with friends, drinking wine, playing music, talking ideas, *always* about ideas."

He continues: "My friends and I wondered, how do we find work here that we love to do? We were learning the ecology of the mountains and we wanted to act to take care of them. We felt that there was something missing in the conservation discussions of the time, and we finally came to the question, How can education play a deep role in conservation by effecting long-term change through changing attitudes?"

Weisberg and Fleischner cofounded North Cascades Institute in 1986 with the mission to conserve and restore Northwest environments through education. "We took people out to special places—the Methow Valley, Harts Pass, Thunder Creek, Cascade Pass—to experience the wild power of the North Cascades," he explains. "It's a thirteen-million-acre ecosystem, with more than seven million acres protected in one form or another on both sides of the border . . . what an amazing classroom, so big and wild!"

The National Park Service and US Forest Service were key partners from the beginning, as Weisberg realized the Institute would focus its work on public lands, "bringing people to places *they* owned, so they go home knowing more, feeling pride of being public lands ambassadors in their communities."

But Weisberg knew there was more work to do.

"As we tried to figure out how we could most effect change—the Institute's unofficial mission is to save the world—we started thinking about reaching kids," Weisberg recalls. "And so began our residential environmental education program Mountain School in 1989 . . . now 70–80 percent of our focus is on young people.

"Being out in field with kids has changed my life," he continues. "I am so impressed by their energy, enthusiasm and love of learning. They have a natural sense of concern and the ability to not blame anyone for our problems. They're like, 'It's our world, so what are *we* going to do with it?' The future generations move forward with such great confidence. It gives me hope."

In the three decades since he sat around a campfire with his friends wondering what "right livelihood" would look like, Weisberg has created a lasting legacy in these mountains, including the Institute's Environmental Learning Center on partnership with the National Park Service and Seattle City Light. With his passion for the North Cascades, his penchant for poetry, philosophy, and naturalizing, Weisberg has unearthed connections between education, inspiration, and conservation to create generations of stewards for the North Cascades.

Kids from Colorado, California, and Washington State gather to photograph a mountain goat spotted on the slopes near Mount Baker.

A North Cascades Institute student in the Youth Leadership Adventures program sets up her tent at Baker Lake. The program features summer opportunities for high school and college-aged students on local public lands. Students canoe, camp, backpack, and complete service projects.

JOHN SCURLOCK
PILOT AND PHOTOGRAPHER

John Scurlock makes his living as a paramedic for the Bellingham Fire Department but finds his calling soaring above the North Cascades in a tiny yellow airplane that he built with his own hands. Flying above the jagged peaks and yawning glaciers of the "American Alps," the upper Skagit Valley resident journeys into this frozen terra incognita and brings back dramatic panoramas of a winter wonderland seldom seen by human eyes.

Scurlock had wanted to be a pilot since childhood and in his thirties began building his own plane from a kit in his garage near Rockport. It took nine years to assemble the tiny twenty-two-foot, two-seat, tail-wheel plane.

His first aerial photographs of the North Cascades came in the 1990s, when he flew over the Picket Range looking at hiking and climbing routes. He began systematic documentation of the North Cascades in 2002, when he photographed Mount Baker for Kevin Scott of the USGS Cascades Volcano Observatory, and soon after when he did the same for David Tucker of Western Washington University's Mount Baker Volcano Research Center. His photos of fumaroles, steam vents, and glaciers have contributed significantly to the understanding of Baker's geologic history.

Mount Baker is often referred to as the Great White Watcher, looming over Whatcom County on the western edge of the North Cascades, and a sea of peaks separated by deep forested river valleys stretches for a hundred miles to the east. While Baker and neighboring Mount Shuksan are photogenic icons admired by millions of people—skiers and snowboarders in the winter, weekend road trippers in the summer, lower British Columbia residents year-round—the wild heart of the range lies out of sight. It was into this ice-bound realm that Scurlock began flying and recording what he saw.

"I started photographing the rest of the range after I realized that I was seeing the mountains in a condition that was really unknown," Scurlock explains. "Photographs of the range in winter either were very limited or didn't exist. That led me to my great obsession."

Scurlock's body of work from the past decade reveals a vast landscape buried in snow and encrusted in ice, a wintery realm of terrifying beauty and austere grace: the frost-tortured north face of Mount Triumph, gravity-defying cornices on Cloudcap Peak, the Picket Range hidden in mist, Ripsaw Ridge and Glacier Peak and Park Creek Pass in snowy, silent repose. This region holds the world's record for most snowfall ever recorded in a single winter, and Scurlock's photography unveils the artistic potential of the seldom-seen landscape, "something primitive, forbidden and inaccessible, yet also profoundly and exquisitely beautiful," according to Scurlock.

His efforts have resulted in a popular book of his photographs, *Snow and Spire: Flights to Winter in the North Cascade Range*, and an avid online following of climbers, backcountry skiers, and others who appreciate his one-of-a-kind perspective.

"I've been enormously privileged to see things that are nearly incomprehensible in their wildness and wonderful aesthetics," he explains. "I've been so fortunate to be in the position to photograph what I've seen and share those images with everyone else. Digital photography and a great airplane are the means to accomplish this, and obsession is the driving force."

Mount Triumph

Volcano researcher David Tucker probes a fumarole inside Sherman Crater on Mount Baker in preparation for volcanic gas sampling.

Volcano researchers David Tucker (Mount Baker Volcano Research Center) and Sarah Polster (US Geological Service) prepare to board a helicopter flown by Anthony Reese of Hi-Line Helicopters of Darrington, Washington. Dave and Sarah spent the day inside Sherman Crater on Mount Baker doing volcanic gas sampling and other research.

GERRY COOK
FIRE LOOKOUT AND NATIONAL PARK SERVICE BUILDER

Being the third generation of Cooks living and working in the North Cascades did not strike Gerry Cook as particularly unusual or special—that is, until his daughter Kerri was born. Now his family history in these mountains has great meaning for him, he says, "because of my daughter not only following in my footsteps but *exceeding* them."

Cook's roots in this landscape reach back to 1924, when his grandfather moved from Seattle to the company town of Newhalem as part of the first wave of Seattle City Light employees. Guy Cook drove the train from Rockport up the Skagit Valley, delivering tourists to admire J. D. Ross's massive hydroelectric project. Gerry's father, Ed Cook, worked at the Marblemount Fish Hatchery, and after graduating from Concrete High School, Gerry found work in the North Cascades too.

Working for the US Forest Service, the federal agency that oversaw the region at the time, he served on a helitack fire response crew and labored on a trail crew in one of the least visited wilderness areas in the country: "I only saw three hikers the whole summer!"

When the North Cascades became a national park in 1968, Cook stayed on, though his first assignment with the National Park Service was one he didn't particularly want: stationed as a fire lookout atop Desolation Peak. It was a post that would change his life forever.

"I spent almost ninety straight days on top of Desolation and only saw seven other people," Cook recalls. "I was twenty-one and had never spent *any* time alone in wilderness. It gave me a lot of time to reflect during some very troubling times in America, to tune out the silly stuff and think about what's important. It was very therapeutic."

For two more summers he returned to what must be one of the loneliest occupations in America, atop Sourdough Mountain and then Copper Ridge. "Copper Ridge was my special place," Cook remembers, "watching the Picket Range change day after day, always the same, always different." By then, he was savvy enough to pack good food, cases of wine, art supplies, and a box of fifty books.

As park operations began to expand, Cook found a new vocation building infrastructure for visitors. For his first project, he designed and constructed the viewing platform at the Newhalem Visitor Center, providing a vista of his beloved Pickets. Over the next fifteen years, Cook built boardwalks, shelters, overlooks, campgrounds, and picnic areas; helped reconfigure all the backcountry sites on Ross Lake; designed a new park entrance on the west side; and lent his skills to creative projects at the North Cascades Institute's Environmental Learning Center.

"Because I grew up here, I had a sense of what's right and what isn't for the area," he explains. "I use natural materials as much as possible, especially cedar and rock. The core of the North Cascades is rock, so I incorporate it into most of my projects."

As his tenure in the North Cascades unfolded, Cook seized on opportunities to work with young people, first in the early 1970s with Student Conservation Association crews—"great kids coming from middle-class backgrounds, smart and worldly"—and later with North Cascades Institute programs for underserved youth.

"These kids were of different ethnicities from all over the world," he explains. "They'd come in nervous and uncomfortable, never having been in the woods before, but soon become a strong family unit, finding deep connections with the wilderness. I could see these kids' lives change right in front of my eyes. When they leave the North Cascades, they've been transformed into stewards of the planet. This is the most important work I can do and I can't get enough of it."

The Cook lineage in these mountains carries on through Kerri, who works in North Cascades National Park's maintenance department like her father. As early as age four, she was tagging along with her dad up Ross Lake on the park's boat the *Ross Mule*, and a favorite childhood activity was stewarding trails and campgrounds with the student crews.

"I'd watch Kerri working so hard, with a big smile on her face, and know that my girl was going to have an incredible work ethic and enjoy physical outside efforts," he reminisces. "She's grown up with 'park in her blood.' I never influenced her to join the National Park Service and it seems like magic to me that she's stuck around and we've been able to work on projects together."

Kerri's job has her traveling to other parks around the country, but, says her proud dad, "she can't wait to get home to these mountains."

A team of volunteers builds a shelter in North Cascades National Park.

The Methow Valley Hand Crew descends a ridge after containing a spot fire at the edge of the 2003 Needles Fire.

The Methow Valley Hand Crew mops up at a lightning fire during initial attack. Drought and warmer temperatures fuel more frequent and intense wildfires.

KASSANDRA BARNEDT

STUDENT AND VOLUNTEER

Raised on a farm in Concrete, Kassandra Barnedt and her younger siblings spent days building forts and taking mud baths. Her father taught her how to bait a hook when she was seven and shoot a rifle at age nine. She learned about her wider neighborhood by hunting grouse and deer up Jackman Creek and fishing for trout on Lake Shannon.

Concrete is a small community of around seven hundred, first platted in 1890 at the junction of the Baker and Skagit rivers. It sits halfway between the bustling Skagit Valley lowlands and the loneliness of the mountains upvalley. Most everyone knows each other, sometimes going back several generations. Barnedt graduated in a high school class of only twenty-three.

Barnedt fondly remembers growing up in a tight-knit community: "We always had adults looking out for us, so it felt like I had more than one set of parents." But she also felt the limitations. "Because I wasn't exposed to that many different ways of living, it felt like my dreams of what I could do were limited," she explains. "Most people I knew worked in traditional careers like logging and fishing, and I sometimes felt stuck, like I didn't know what else I could strive toward."

Though Barnedt spent most of her early years in the foothills of the North Cascades, it wasn't until she was fifteen that she really got to know her wild backyard. A park ranger's

presentation to her junior class inspired her to sign up for the North Cascades Institute's twelve-day backcountry program that teaches high school students about stewardship, wilderness skills, and leadership.

"I wanted the challenge of spending two weeks with people who came from somewhere other than my hometown," she explains, "to hang out with teenagers who have different perspectives." Barnedt's group of eight happened to all be girls, including teens recently immigrated from Ethiopia, Gambia, and Mexico.

The group backpacked and canoed on Ross Lake, and the wilderness, so new to the girls, brought them together quickly. "Living together 24/7 with no private space, sleeping in the same tents, preparing food together, learning outdoor skills none of us had ever done . . . we dropped being shy and got honest and open with each other," Barnedt recalls. "It got deep pretty quick." Some opened up about troubled family lives, others about leaving their home countries and trying to establish new roots.

It wasn't all talking and tears though. The young women dug into stewardship work such as brushing trail, building tread, and moving windfallen trees. Their days were full of physical labor and they had to figure out how to work together as a team:

"Everything was so large and we were so small!"

When Barnedt returned home, she had made a significant shift.

"I got a lot more courage and became more outspoken. 'It's OK to love nature,' I told myself, 'and spending time in it *is* valuable.'"

The experience changed Barnedt's life trajectory too. She decided to pursue a degree in environmental education, landed a position at the Marblemount Native Plant Nursery with the Youth Conservation Corps for two summers, and then was hired by the national park's maintenance department.

"How can we make environmental issues personal, make them matter, to students my age?" Barnedt asks. "Ideally everyone would get the opportunity to spend time in the wilderness, but you don't *have* to go canoeing for two weeks; we can start here at home, in our neighborhoods and our schools."

To that end, Barnedt has led campground cleanups and has taken local high school students to popular Cascade Pass to plant kinnikinnick and mountain heather where thousands of hiking boots have trampled the fragile alpine ecosystem. And she began recruiting the next generation of North Cascades Institute participants from Skagit Valley schools. "Being able to share my stories with students while wearing the official green park uniform," she recalls, "that was really cool."

Barnedt's outlook for her generation is upbeat: "It's hard to be discouraged when you live so close to beautiful places, working with such amazing people. Spending time in the North Cascades is a constant refuel for me. I think that if we're really determined to change things for the better, there will be doors that open for us. We can't get defeated. We need to keep moving forward."

A park ranger shares stories with North Cascades Institute's Mountain School students.

WASHINGTON TRAILS ASSOCIATION (WTA) fields Washington State's largest volunteer trail maintenance program. In addition, the organization educates and promotes hiking opportunities, and advocates on behalf of hikers to support increased funding for trails. Above, WTA volunteers slide one of the final pieces of a new bridge over Early Winters Creek into place. The broken bridge in the water is one of many old bridges that have surpassed their life expectancy and need to be replaced on trails in the Methow.

STUDENT CONSERVATION ASSOCIATION (SCA) volunteers are crucial to maintaining park resources, and many SCA alumni use their experience to launch careers at North Cascades and other national parks.

The Loomis State Forest of 134,000 acres in Okanogan county provides important habitat for wildlife and is one of the most important places for the federally listed lynx in the lower forty-eight states. Other rare carnivores, including wolverines and fishers also call the Loomis home.

In 1999, preservationists successfully raised $16.5 million to buy twenty-five thousand acres of old-growth wilderness and sub-alpine meadows. More than 3,500 individuals across the state donated money, including a generous last-minute "save" from philanthropist and Microsoft founder Paul Allen.

Logging supports school-trust funds for school construction, and the money raised in the preservation campaign has been used to benefit schools and compensate the trust for the loss of logging revenues. The Loomis State Forest is now managed by the Department of Natural Resources to benefit all the people of Washington. Recreational uses include snowmobiling, horse-packing and hiking, and cattlemen may still use the land for grazing. The protections prohibit logging and roadbuilding.

In the late twentieth century, the northern spotted owl became the centerpiece of a bitter battle between environmentalists and the logging industry. It received legal protection via the Endangered Species Act, and became a national symbol for a key environmental issue: whether to log or preserve old-growth forests of the Pacific Northwest.

In a perverse twist of fate, the spotted owl faces a new battle with extinction. The new threat comes from an invasion of its last territories from one of its own cousins—the highly adaptable and aggressive barred owl.

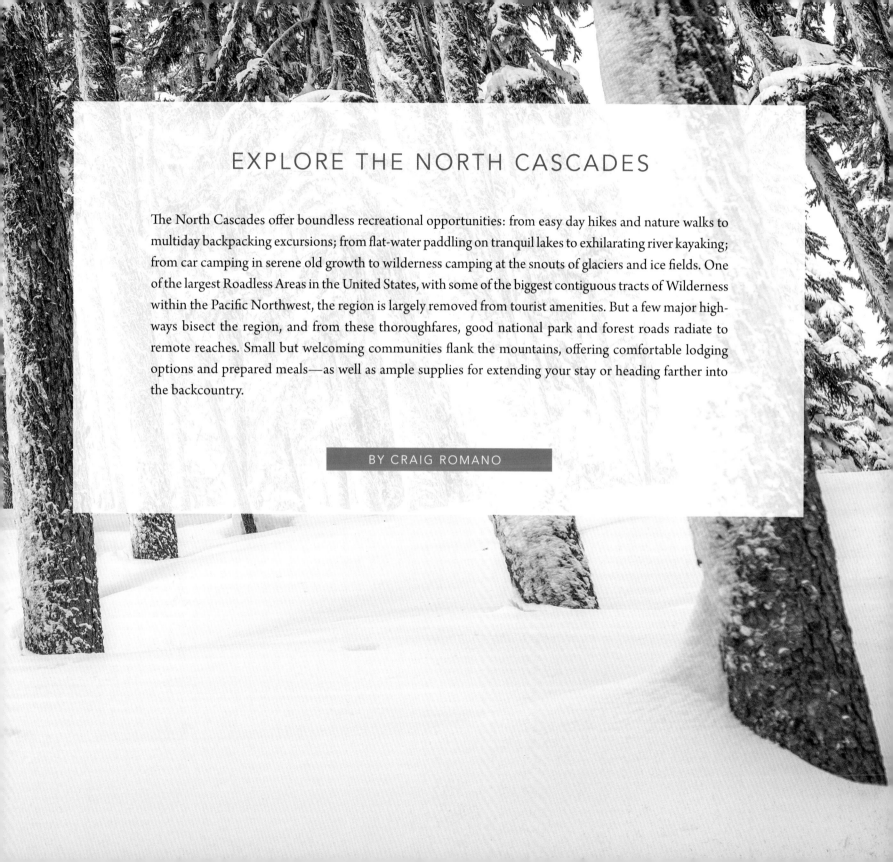

EXPLORE THE NORTH CASCADES

The North Cascades offer boundless recreational opportunities: from easy day hikes and nature walks to multiday backpacking excursions; from flat-water paddling on tranquil lakes to exhilarating river kayaking; from car camping in serene old growth to wilderness camping at the snouts of glaciers and ice fields. One of the largest Roadless Areas in the United States, with some of the biggest contiguous tracts of Wilderness within the Pacific Northwest, the region is largely removed from tourist amenities. But a few major highways bisect the region, and from these thoroughfares, good national park and forest roads radiate to remote reaches. Small but welcoming communities flank the mountains, offering comfortable lodging options and prepared meals—as well as ample supplies for extending your stay or heading farther into the backcountry.

BY CRAIG ROMANO

Photographing balsamroot in the Methow Valley

Harts Pass area in the Okanogan–Wenatchee National Forest

North Cascades National Park offers plenty of hiking options.

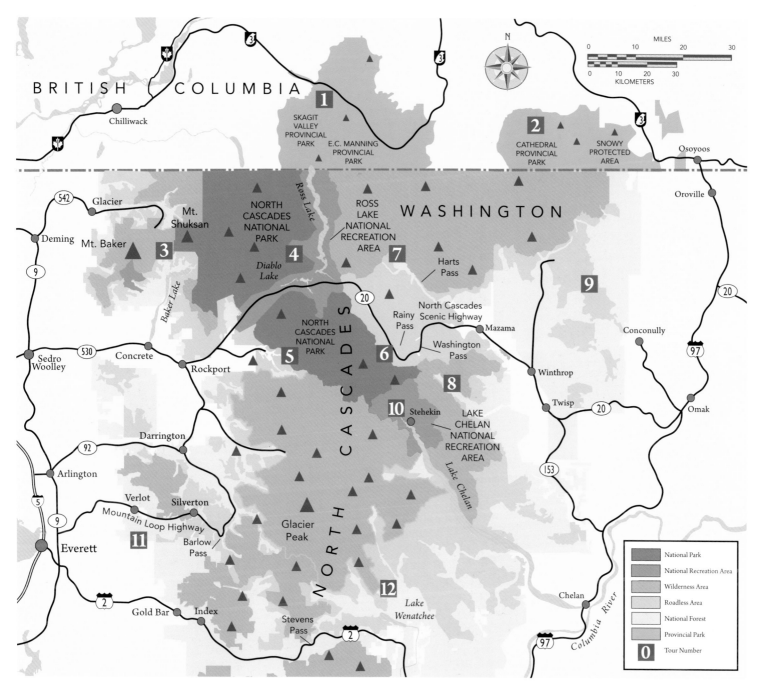

Explore the North Cascades: Twelve Tours

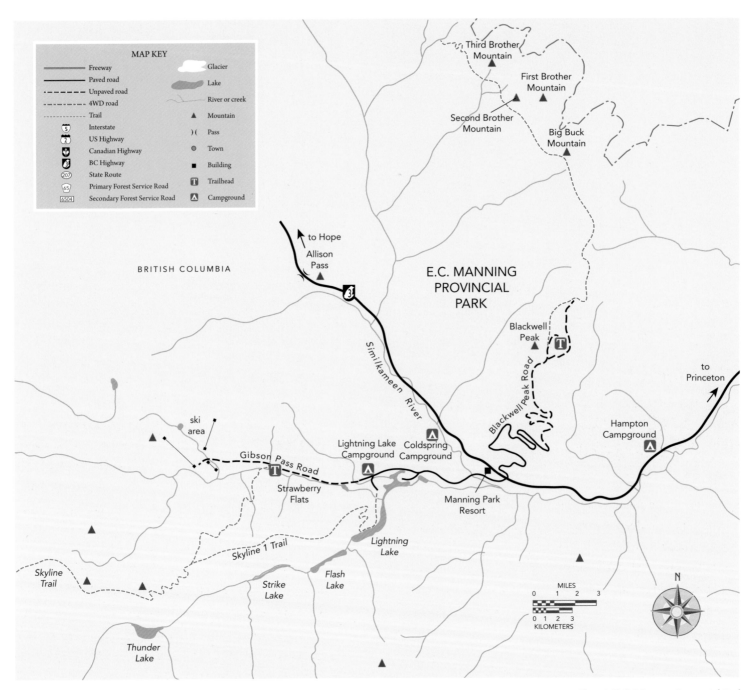

Tour 1. E.C. Manning Provincial Park

THE NORTH CASCADES cover a vast ecoregion containing geographically distinct groupings of natural communities and species, from interior rain forest to shrub-steppe, alpine tundra to deciduous and coniferous forests. What follows are a dozen of the finest areas within the North Cascades for you to explore and personally experience. They were chosen for their accessibility, exceptional and diverse recreational opportunities, and for their variety of life zones and ecosystems. Also various are the land management agencies and classifications represented: a national park, national forests, national recreation areas, wilderness areas, state parks, and provincial parks. Each area is a distinct section of this enormous region. Taken together, they display the remarkable biological and geographical diversity that this landscape offers—and the unlimited recreational opportunities that await you.

1. EXPLORE: E.C. MANNING PROVINCIAL PARK
HOPE, BRITISH COLUMBIA

Sprawling alpine meadows, unbroken tracts of ancient forest, soaring summits, deep valleys, rushing rivers, and placid lakes: British Columbia's E. C. Manning Provincial Park captures the full essence of the North Cascades' northern reaches. A transition zone between wet coastal mountains and dry interior plateaus, Manning supports a wide array of wildlife, including threatened northern spotted owls and grizzly bears. Two of the North Cascades' biggest rivers, the west-flowing Skagit and the east-flowing Similkameen, originate in this more than 175,000-acre park. Along with the adjacent Skagit Valley Provincial Park and, in the United States, the Pasayten Wilderness, Manning forms the core of one of the North Cascades' largest protected areas. With the Crowsnest Highway (Highway 3) bisecting the park, a lodge, several campgrounds, nearly 200 miles of hiking and ski trails, and downhill skiing, Manning is also one of the North Cascades' most accessible and popular areas.

HIKE: THREE BROTHERS MOUNTAIN
Walk along a lofty, gentle rolling ridge through clumps of tenacious subalpine firs and sprawling meadows that blossom in a riot of colors. Don't let the full roundtrip mileage dissuade you: you start at nearly 6,600 feet and gain little elevation, and you don't have to hike very far for scenic rewards—as flowering

Young black bears require room to roam—and climb.

meadows greet you at the trailhead. But if the Three Brothers are your objective (there are three distinct summits), follow the Heather Trail across the subalpine wonderland reaches of Big Buck Mountain to the 7,450-foot First Brother. Then scan the landscape from southwest to northeast, noting the jagged snow-clad summits enveloped in emerald swaths that then yield to drier, piney broad plateaus. **Roundtrip:** *13 miles.* **Elevation gain:** *1,575 feet.* **Difficulty:** *Easy to moderate.* **Trailhead:** *Blackwell Peak Road end, 9.3 miles from Manning Park Resort.*

HIKE: SKYLINE TRAILS

Two of the finest ridge-hugging routes in the North Cascades, Skyline I and Skyline II trails meander along a high divide carpeted in wildflower-bursting meadows, surrounded by snow-capped summits, and burgeoning with wildlife. Stare straight down at Thunder Lake wedged between steep slopes stripped of vegetation from an endless procession of avalanches. And look south to the colossal pyramids of the Pasayten Wilderness— and to the stark rocky spires of Hozomeen Mountain, which entranced poet Jack Kerouac during his stint as a fire lookout on Desolation Peak in the summer of 1956. **Roundtrip:** *Up to 20 miles.* **Elevation gain:** *Up to 2,500 feet.* **Difficulty:** *Moderate to difficult.* **Trailheads:** *Near Lightning Lake Campground or Strawberry Flats, on Gibson Pass Road.*

SKI

Manning Provincial Park is a winter recreation wonderland, with a lift-serviced downhill ski area, a Nordic area offering groomed trails, and a system of backcountry ski trails.

PADDLE

Canoe or kayak on motor-free Lightning Lake, nestled near the park's center. Cast for trout. Watch for moose, beaver, and the occasional loon enjoying the surrounding verdant slopes. Consider the short portage to Flash Lake for more peaceful paddling.

CAR CAMPING

Choose from 350 sites in four developed campgrounds within the park. The Lightning Lake Campground is the most popular, offering reservations, hot showers, and beach access.

PARK LODGE

Stay at the Manning Park Resort in a lodge room or cabin. Located just east of 4,403-foot Allison Pass in the middle of the park and open year-round, the resort also offers food service and canoe, kayak, ski, and snowshoe rentals.

2. EXPLORE: CATHEDRAL PROVINCIAL PARK
KEREMEOS, BRITISH COLUMBIA

Cathedral Provincial Park protects more than 83,000 acres of unbroken forests, a series of alpine lakes tucked within dramatic cirques, peaks rising more than 8,000 feet, and fascinating rock formations. Located between the windswept alpine tundra plains of the Pasayten Wilderness and the sweltering sunbaked

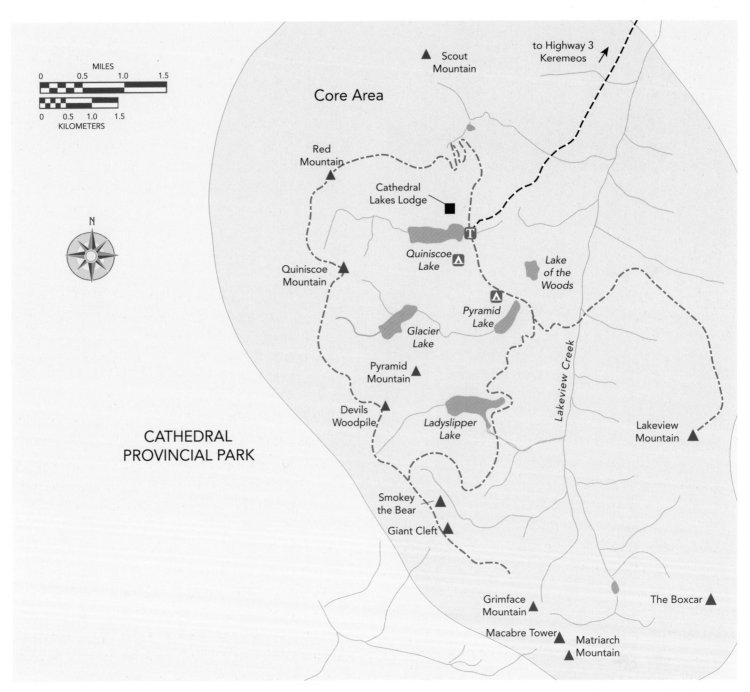

MILES
0   0.5   1.0   1.5

KILOMETERS
0   0.5   1.0   1.5

N

CATHEDRAL
PROVINCIAL PARK

Core Area

▲ Scout
Mountain

to Highway 3
Keremeos

Red
Mountain ▲

Cathedral
Lakes Lodge ■

T

Quiniscoe
Lake

Lake
of the
Woods

Quiniscoe
Mountain ▲

Pyramid
Lake

Glacier
Lake

Lakeview Creek

Pyramid
Mountain ▲

Devils
Woodpile ▲

Ladyslipper
Lake

Lakeview
Mountain ▲

Smokey
the Bear ▲

Giant Cleft ▲

Grimface
Mountain ▲

The Boxcar ▲

Macabre Tower ▲

Matriarch
Mountain ▲

Tour 2. Cathedral Provincial Park

Camping under the stars

lichen-encrusted cairns to summits exceeding 8,300 feet in elevation. Admire a half-dozen alpine lakes twinkling below in cliffy amphitheaters carved by ice age glaciers. Savor views of the Pasayten Wilderness's towering peaks and marvel at fascinating rock formations along the rim: the Devils Woodpile, an outcropping of columnar basalt; Stone City, rounded rocks resembling giant curling stones piled atop each other; Smokey the Bear, a large sheer cliff face; and the Giant Cleft. **Roundtrip:** *Up to 8 miles.* **Elevation gain:** *Up to 2,000 feet.* **Difficulty:** *Moderate to difficult.* **Trailhead:** *Quiniscoe Lake.*

HIKE: LAKEVIEW MOUNTAIN

Descend from Quiniscoe Lake, passing lovely Pyramid Lake before crossing Lakeview Creek. Then grind upward through pine, fir, and larch forest, emerging on broad, massive Lakeview Mountain. At 8,622 feet, it's the highest summit in the park and its views are unsurpassed. Look back at the Cathedral Rim, with its shiny granite arêtes and deep cirques cradling sparkling lakes. Look south into the Pasayten country, with its golden tundra plains punctuated by abrupt summits. And look east to expansive 8,494-foot Snowy Mountain rising 7,000 feet above the Similkameen Valley, one of the grandest trenches in the North Cascades. **Roundtrip:** *7 miles.* **Elevation gain:** *2,300 feet.* **Difficulty:** *Moderate.* **Trailhead:** *Quiniscoe Lake.*

HISTORICAL INTEREST

Keremeos Grist Mill is located in the town of Keremeos in the Similkameen Valley. It was built in 1877 to produce flour from First Nations' wheat to supply area prospectors. A British Columbia heritage site, the mill grounds include original equipment, a museum, gardens, and historical orchard.

steppe of the Similkameen Valley, Cathedral boasts flora and fauna as diverse as its landscapes. Mountain goats, ptarmigans, bighorn sheep, badgers, grizzly bears, lynx, and prairie falcons all take refuge within this wilderness park. Except for a private rough jeep track accessing a lodge and campgrounds at Quiniscoe Lake, the park is roadless. Visitors can pay to be shuttled to the park's center or can backpack 10 long and steep miles from the valley below.

HIKE: CATHEDRAL RIM

Four trails ranging in difficulty ascend the rocky open ridges and summits forming the Cathedral Rim. Clamber through scree, over boulder fields, and across alpine tundra following

WILDERNESS CAMPING

There are three wilderness campgrounds with tent pads, picnic tables, and privies within the park's core at Pyramid Lake, Quiniscoe Lake, and Lake of the Woods. Backpack to them or arrange for a shuttle pickup through the Cathedral Lakes Lodge.

CATHEDRAL LAKES LODGE

Located on Quiniscoe Lake within the park's core, at an elevation of 6,800 feet, this full-service lodge, the highest in Canada, allows visitors to experience the surrounding wilderness in comfort. From the lodge, guests can day hike to the park's highest reaches or take one of the lodge's canoes out for a paddle.

---

3. EXPLORE: HEATHER MEADOWS
GLACIER, MOUNT BAKER–SNOQUALMIE NATIONAL FOREST

Follow the Mount Baker Highway (State Route 542), a spectacularly scenic national byway, to Heather Meadows, a subalpine world of resplendent wildflowers, hemlock-hugging hillocks, and gleaming lakes set beneath barren slopes perpetually cloaked in snow and ice. Tucked between two North Cascades iconic peaks, 9,131-foot Mount Shuksan (one of the most photographed mountains in the country) and 10,781-foot Mount Baker (Washington's third-highest and snowiest summit), this high bench is easily accessible by automobile. Paved wheelchair-accessible paths and well-groomed trails radiate across the meadows, inviting more intimate explorations—be it easy

ambling with camera and tripod or challenging clambering with ice ax in hand and a summit in mind.

HIKE: CHAIN LAKES

Loop around snow- and ice-clad Table Mountain to a half-dozen alpine lakes harboring mini icebergs well into fall. Delight in summer blossoms, autumn berries, and year-round scenic splendor—especially southwest to Baker and east to Shuksan, two frosty bookend giants. From the Bagley Lakes beneath Table Mountain's columnar cliffs of ancient lava, climb to 5,400-foot Herman Saddle and its knock-your-sunglasses-off views. Then drop into old-growth forest to the Chain Lakes before climbing to a stark 5,200-foot gap with stunning views of Ptarmigan Ridge's ice and tundra. From there, traverse open slopes carpeted

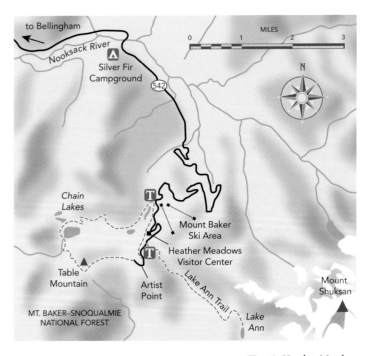

Tour 3. Heather Meadows

Flaming mountain-ash, Mount Shuksan

Sunrise on Lake Ann beneath Mount Shuksan

in crimson come September to Artist Point, following the Wild Goose Trail back to your start. **Roundtrip:** *7 miles.* **Elevation gain:** *1,600 feet.* **Difficulty:** *Moderate.* **Trailhead:** *Upper ski area parking lot or Heather Meadows Visitor Center.*

HIKE: LAKE ANN

Traverse primeval forest, flowering meadows, lush bogs, and shiny talus slopes to Lake Ann cradled in a high basin beneath 9,131-foot Mount Shuksan. Ann's dark blue-green waters, oft-ringed in snow, reflect an awesome backdrop of craggy glacier-clad spires. Start with a long descent into the Swift Creek valley, dropping 900 feet. Then regain your lost elevation, climbing to a small saddle above the open basin that embraces shimmering Lake Ann. Gaze across its chilling waters to Mount Shuksan, watching blocks of ice from hanging glaciers break away and crash to the valley below. The Skagit peoples named Shuksan, and it means "roaring mountain." Apropos indeed. **Roundtrip:** *8.2 miles.* **Elevation gain:** *1,900 feet.* **Difficulty:** *Moderate.* **Trailhead:** *Austin Pass, about 1 mile beyond Heather Meadows Visitor Center.*

SNOWSHOE: ARTIST POINT

The road to Artist Point, which is oft blanketed in snow ten months of the year, makes an excellent snowshoe trip. Trudge up open slopes to the lofty perch on a shoulder smack dab between Mounts Baker and Shuksan. On easel or memory card, capture the stunning snowy surroundings. Come on an evening during a full moon, and swear you've reached heaven, albeit a frosty version. **Roundtrip:** *4 miles.* **Elevation gain:** *1,100 feet.* **Difficulty:** *Moderate.* **Trailhead:** *Mount Baker Ski Area upper parking lot.*

HISTORICAL INTEREST

Heather Meadows Visitor Center sits on a rock ledge overlooking the snow-fed Bagley Lakes. Elegantly rustic, it was constructed as a ski warming hut by the Civilian Conservation Corps in 1940. It now provides historical interpretation and outdoor recreation information during the summer.

CAR CAMPING

Nestled in primeval forest on the banks of the roaring North Fork of the Nooksack River, find the family-friendly Douglas Fir Campground, developed long ago by the Civilian Conservation Corps, and the more private Silver Fir Campground.

4. EXPLORE: ROSS LAKE AND SKAGIT RIVER
MARBLEMOUNT, ROSS LAKE NATIONAL RECREATION AREA, NORTH CASCADES NATIONAL PARK COMPLEX

Born of snow and ice, the Skagit River flows about 150 miles on its way to the Salish Sea. The Skagit is the third-largest watershed on the west coast of the continental United States, and not one major city sits upon its banks. Its headwaters remain untrammeled and wild, and most of its course runs free—except its midsection, which was altered by a series of dams creating Gorge, Diablo, and Ross lakes, the latter in essence an inland fjord.

In late summer, finely ground rock particles, or glacial flour, and the lake's water absorb all colors of the light spectrum except those that create the opaque turquoise seen in Diablo Lake.

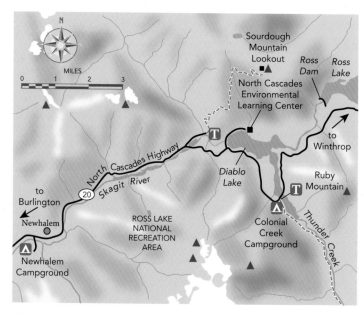

Tour 4. Ross Lake and Skagit River

Cloud-wringing peaks form a rain shadow, allowing for the growth of pine, birch, and other species that generally favor the east side of the Cascade Crest. Here they flourish among the cedars, hemlocks, and Douglas firs. This transitional forest is rich in biological diversity and makes for a stunning outdoor laboratory. It's the perfect setting for the North Cascades Institute's Environmental Learning Center, which sits on the banks of Diablo Lake surrounded by glacier-capped summits.

HIKE: SOURDOUGH MOUNTAIN

Gaining more than 1 vertical mile in just over 5 linear miles, the trail to Sourdough Mountain is one of the most challenging in the North Cascades. And it's one of the most stunning. From its brilliant alpine meadows shrouded in wildflowers, stare straight down to the glacier-fed turquoise waters of Diablo Lake. Then revel in a panorama of seemingly endless waves of ice-capped emerald peaks, whose jagged summits snag passing clouds. Admire Sourdough's recently restored fire lookout, originally built in 1933, where poets Philip Whalen and Gary Snyder both worked stints in the 1950s. No shortage of inspiration from this post. **Roundtrip:** *11 miles.* **Elevation gain:** *5,100 feet.* **Difficulty:** *Difficult.* **Trailhead:** *Behind tennis courts in Diablo, just off North Cascades Highway (State Route 20).*

HIKE: THUNDER CREEK

Hike for a few hours or a few days along a bellowing tributary of the Skagit River into one of the deepest, wildest wilderness valleys in the North Cascades. Saunter through groves of monstrous ancient cedars and towering firs. Reflect upon the hardscrabble prospectors who once funneled into this green hole looking for fortunes. And admire the wealth of wildlife—deer, bears, bobcats, cougars, and owls that prance, prowl, and prey in this ancient valley. **Roundtrip:** *Up to 32 miles.* **Elevation gain:** *Up to 4,000 feet.* **Difficulty:** *Easy to difficult.* **Trailhead:** *Colonial Creek Campground.*

PADDLE

Paddle the stunningly blue-green and calm waters of Diablo Lake. Venture into the tight rock-walled Skagit Canyon or forest-flanked Thunder Arm. Or paddle Ross Lake, a majestic 24-mile-long inland fjord to hidden coves, crashing waterfalls, rocky islands, and viewpoints of surrounding soaring summits. Backcountry shoreline campsites will entice you to stay awhile.

If you would like to experience the free-flowing section of the Skagit River you can paddle the whitewater stretch downstream of Newhalem through the class III S-Bends, or put-in farther

A cedar waxwing perches among the berries of a saskatoon.

down to experience a more mellow float on a segment known for the hundreds of eagles that come to the river each winter.

NATURE WALKS

Choose from among a delightful assortment of short nature and interpretive walks in and around Newhalem. Walk along the Skagit River and cross over it on a suspension bridge. Visit a waterfall, big cedars, a manicured garden, an inspiring view of the forbidding Picket Range, and an aboriginal 1,400-year-old rock shelter once used as a hunting camp.

HISTORICAL INTEREST

Stop at the Skagit General Store in Newhalem and take the walking tour around this company town that began in 1918 as a construction camp and then housed employees working on the area's hydroelectric dams.

CAR CAMPING

Pitch your tent at Colonial Creek Campground, nestled in magnificent old-growth forest along the shores of Diablo Lake; or at the Newhalem Campground on the Skagit River, within walking distance of the North Cascades National Park Visitor Center and the historic company town of Newhalem.

VISIT, STAY, LEARN

The nonprofit North Cascades Institute's Environmental Learning Center on the shores of Diablo Lake is open to learners of all ages. Operated in partnership with the Seattle City Light and the National Park Service, the forested campus includes multimedia classrooms, aquatic and terrestrial labs, a lakeside dining hall, lodging for ninety-two participants, hiking trails, and wheelchair-accessible pathways.

5. EXPLORE: CASCADE RIVER VALLEY
MARBLEMOUNT, NORTH CASCADES NATIONAL PARK

One of the great rivers of the North Cascades, the Cascade drains an amazing array of glacier-clad summits into one of the largest roadless areas in the continental United States. A major tributary to the Skagit, this national wild and scenic river tumbles through a dramatic U-shaped glaciated valley saturated by ample rainfall. One of the wettest corners of the North Cascades, this river valley is lined with massive cedars, maples,

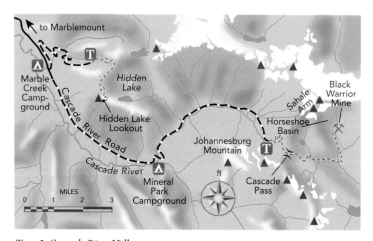

Tour 5. Cascade River Valley

Star trails above the Hidden Lake Lookout

firs, and hemlocks cloaked in mosses and lichens. This corridor was long used by First Peoples, explorers, traders, miners, and settlers as a route across the mountains. Now a good paved and gravel road winds 23 miles along the pristine river, providing the only drive-in access to the North Cascades National Park.

HIKE: CASCADE PASS

From a lofty start at the edge of an avalanche chute beneath the fierce face of 8,200-foot Johannesburg Mountain, follow a route used by Native Americans, explorers, prospectors, and survey-ors to reach Lake Chelan. This well-traveled, relatively low pass was once considered by railroad and highway engineers. But the railroad never came, and the highway went north: now this area is protected as wilderness within North Cascades National Park.

The well-built and nicely graded trail switchbacks some thirty times before making a long traverse across heather meadows, talus, and lingering snowfields to 5,400-foot Cascade Pass. Marvel at a formidable wall of imposing peaks decked with hanging glaciers that occasionally send ice crashing below. Admire, too, the Stehekin Valley to the east and Cascade River valley to the west. **Roundtrip:** *7.4 miles.* **Elevation gain:** *1,800 feet.* **Difficulty:** *Moderate.* **Trailhead:** *Cascade River Road end.*

HIKE: HIDDEN LAKE LOOKOUT

Traverse sprawling alpine meadows, granite slabs, and glisten-ing snowfields to reach a historical fire lookout precariously perched on a craggy 6,890-foot thumb. Stare straight down at shimmering Hidden Lake cradled in a rugged half-frozen hanging valley. Then turn your gaze upward and outward to the serrated skyline of snow and ice. In late summer, flowering heather and batches of glacier lilies help brighten Hidden Lake Peaks' harsh alpine tundra. Clucking ptarmigans, peeping pipits, and soft alpine breezes contribute to a soothing and intriguing soundscape. **Roundtrip:** *9 miles.* **Elevation gain:** *3,200 feet.* **Difficulty:** *Difficult.* **Trailhead:** *Drive Cascade River Road, turn left on Sibley Creek Road (Forest Road 1540), drive 4.7 miles.*

FLY-FISH

Cast for steelhead, rainbow, cutthroat, and Dolly Varden in this tributary of the Skagit. The Cascade River is regularly stocked with steelhead and can be fished during winter and summer runs. There is excellent access from the River Walk near the Marblemount bridge at the Cascade's confluence with the Skagit.

HISTORICAL INTEREST

The Cascade Pass area teems with old mines and is littered with debris from mineral rushes from as far back as the 1890s. The Black Warrior Mine (listed on the National Register of Historic Places) is located in Horseshoe Basin, a huge cirque fed by a half-dozen waterfalls. Explore at will, but don't venture beyond the shaft's entrance. You'll need to backpack to reach the basin and mine, located 8.8 miles from the Cascade Pass trailhead.

CAR CAMPING

Marble Creek and Mineral Park campgrounds, both set in deep timber along the Cascade River, make good family-friendly bases for exploring the valley. Bring your own water.

6. EXPLORE: WASHINGTON PASS AND RAINY PASS

NORTH CASCADES HIGHWAY, OKANOGAN–WENATCHEE NATIONAL FOREST

Completed in 1972, the North Cascades Highway (State Route 20) is one of the most scenic stretches of pavement ever laid in America and one of only two roadways in Washington to cross the North Cascades. Follow this national scenic byway on a

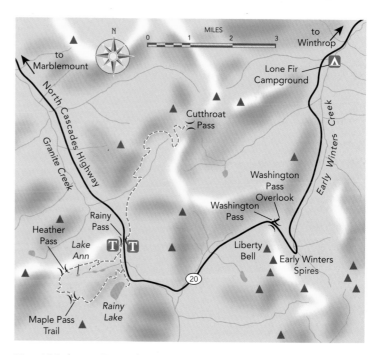

Tour 6. Washington Pass and Rainy Pass

Cinnamon-colored black bear at Maple Pass in the North Cascades. Despite their name, many black bears' coats range from almost white to dark brown. Grizzlies are distinguished by a prominent hump between the shoulders, a dished face, and long claws.

Fishing for salmon

transitional journey over two mountain passes, from rain-saturated valleys to sunny sage-steppe hills. Treacherous avalanche chutes close the road from around late November to mid-April. But when open, this wilderness portal provides easy access to a wide range of trails, campgrounds, scenic overlooks, and visitor centers. From Newhalem to Mazama, a distance of 66 miles, there are no services. It's as wild as a highway can be.

HIKE: CUTTHROAT PASS

Starting at an elevation of 4,800 feet, follow the Pacific Crest Trail through deep forest, across crashing creeks and heather meadows to broad, open 6,837-foot Cutthroat Pass. Straddling the Cascade Crest that separates the wet west and the dry east, Cutthroat supports a wealth of animal and plant diversity. Whistling marmots, shrilling ground squirrels, wallowing mountain goats, and *kraaking* Clark's nutcrackers drawn to the pass's whitebark pines are all common sights. Views are superb too. From snow-shrouded peaks west to sun-kissed summits east, jagged giants encircle you. In autumn, larches add a brilliant golden hue to Cutthroat's granitic ledges. **Roundtrip:** *10 miles.* **Elevation gain:** *1,900 feet.* **Difficulty:** *Moderate.* **Trailhead:** *North Cascades Highway (State Route 20) at Rainy Pass.*

HIKE: MAPLE PASS

This breathtaking loop traverses various life zones, starting in lush old-growth coniferous forest and culminating in alpine tundra. Following the loop, consider the short side trip to shimmering Lake Ann, tucked within a cirque laced with cascades. Continue upward to Heather Pass in the subalpine zone. Then cross snowfields and rock gardens, meandering along the cirque rim to Maple Pass. Lake Ann glistens 1,000 feet directly below.

A Clark's nutcracker looks for food from the top of a subalpine fir in North Cascades National Park.

After cresting a shoulder of Frisco Mountain at 6,850 feet and taking in a breathtaking panoramic view of the snowy, rocky spires, steeply descend to a hanging valley and then rapidly lose more elevation, returning to the trailhead. **Roundtrip:** *7.2 miles.* **Elevation gain:** *2,000 feet.* **Difficulty:** *Moderate.* **Trailhead:** *North Cascades Highway (State Route 20) at Rainy Pass Picnic Area.*

BIKE

Cycle the North Cascades Highway (State Route 20) solo or as part of an organized group. A wide shoulder, good grade, moderate traffic flow, and plenty of places to pull over help make this challenging bike ride along one of America's most scenic roadways attainable and a superb way to absorb the majesty of the North Cascades. At the end of the winter season, after the snowplows have been through but before the road is officially open, there's a brief window when you can have a stretch of the highway all to yourself, no cars at all.

WHEELCHAIR-ACCESSIBLE

From Rainy Pass follow a nearly level 0.9-mile paved path to Rainy Lake, quite possibly the most stunning ADA trail in Washington. This waterfall-fed subalpine lake is nestled in an open cirque beneath formidable 7,780-foot Frisco Mountain.

NATURE WALKS

Stretch your legs near Ross Lake in the Happy Creek Forest along the short wheelchair-accessible boardwalk that leads through a dark forest cheerfully enhanced by a bubbly creek. Stop too at the short paved path at the Washington Pass Overlook to admire quintessential North Cascades peaks, Liberty Bell Mountain and the Early Winters Spires.

HISTORICAL INTEREST

Long before the highway punched through, the now tranquil Ruby Creek Trail near Ross Lake saw its share of activity as a mining district. Claims, mines, and cabins lined the way. Life was tough here: many a doughty fortune seeker left empty-handed. One hardy soul, George Holmes, a former slave, stayed for over thirty years. His pits, along with other old digs, dilapidated structures, and rusting equipment, are still visible along the trail. **Trailhead:** *East Bank trailhead, at milepost 138 on the North Cascades Highway (State Route 20).*

CAR CAMPING

Lone Fir Campground is set along crashing Early Winters Creek in a high valley beneath towering spires. Klipchuck Campground is located downstream, toward Winthrop, in old-growth ponderosa pines and backed by sage-scented hills. Both make great base camps.

7. EXPLORE: HARTS PASS
MAZAMA, OKANOGAN–WENATCHEE NATIONAL FOREST

Drive the highest road in Washington, twisting up steep mountainsides through subalpine forest and alpine meadows to just below the 7,440-foot summit of Slate Peak. Built in 1890s for narrow-gauge vehicles to reach nearby gold and silver mines, the gravel road has been upgraded since and is quite safe, but it's still a somewhat rough and harrowing drive for some modern explorers. Take your time and you'll be fine. And spend some time at Harts Pass exploring remnants from the area's mining history and walking along high ridges easily accessed from lofty trailheads. The views—from glacier-carved valleys to the snowy Cascade Crest to the Pasayten Wilderness—are phenomenal. The summer wildflower display of nearly two hundred species

Aspen grove in the Methow Valley. Aspens typically grow as clones from a single seedling, and spread through long-lived root systems up to thousands of years in age.

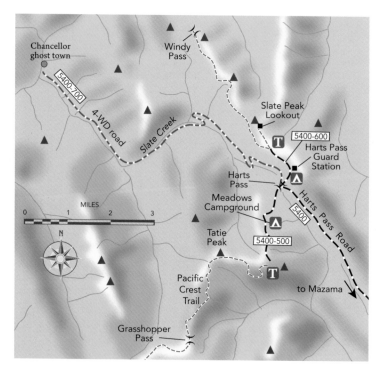

Tour 7. Harts Pass

is dazzling. And autumn's fiery reds and brilliant golds—compliments of larches, aspens, and blueberry bushes—are a sight to behold.

HIKE: WINDY PASS

From the 6,750-foot trailhead, follow the Pacific Crest Trail north on a high ridgeline to 6,257-foot Windy Pass. Skirt beneath Slate Peak with its signature fire tower; and walk along the rim of a basin that once bustled with prospectors. The way winds and dips and gently climbs through parkland forest and across rapturous alpine gardens. Look out upon endless columns of icy and rocky spiraling peaks, separated by deep dark valleys and emerald ridges. **Roundtrip:** *7 miles.* **Elevation gain:** *1,400 feet.*

Difficulty: *Easy to moderate.* **Trailhead:** *Forest Road 5400-600, 1.4 miles beyond Harts Pass.*

HIKE: TATIE PEAK AND GRASSHOPPER PASS

This is one of the finest ridge-running, cloud-probing, peak-peering hikes in the North Cascades—and it's achieved with minimal effort. Starting high and staying high, follow the Pacific Crest Trail south on a rolling course that grants continuous horizon-spanning views of jagged ridges and colossal summits. Amble past an old mine and round high basins harboring squeaky ground squirrels and whistling marmots. Scramble up 7,386-foot Tatie Peak to marvel at clusters of formidable neighboring peaks. Then wander through larch groves, boulder fields, and rock gardens to 6,800-foot Grasshopper Pass, where you can admire a prominent pair of pointy peaks, the Golden Horn and Tower Peak. **Roundtrip:** *11 miles.* **Elevation gain:** *1,800 feet.* **Difficulty:** *Moderate.* **Trailhead:** *Forest Road 5400-500, 2 miles beyond Harts Pass.*

MOUNTAIN BIKE: SLATE CREEK

Follow Forest Road 5400-700, an old road built by miners over a century ago, down into the Slate Creek canyon to the ghost town of Chancellor. At one time, more than a thousand hardscrabble folks lived in this valley, working at several mines and claims. Plenty of relics lie strewn about. **Roundtrip:** *21 miles.* **Elevation gain:** *3,400 feet.* **Difficulty:** *Difficult.* **Trailhead:** *Harts Pass Guard Station.*

HISTORICAL INTEREST

Walk just 0.25 mile to the 41-foot fire lookout atop 7,440-foot Slate Peak. The summit was formerly 40 feet higher, but the US

A family camper van glows at night in the Mineral Park Campground, Mount Baker–Snoqualmie National Forest.

Air Force flattened the mountain in the 1950s to build a radar station here. The radar was never installed and a new tower was built in 1956 to replace the one earlier removed.

CAR CAMPING

Harts Pass Campground sits at 6,200 feet amid subalpine forest near a historical guard station. Meadows Campground is a bit south of the pass, at 6,300 feet on an open knoll. Both offer excellent wildlife watching and superb star gazing. Bring your own water.

8. EXPLORE: TWISP RIVER VALLEY AND SAWTOOTH RIDGE
TWISP, OKANOGAN–WENATCHEE NATIONAL FOREST

A major tributary of the Methow River, the Twisp River flows through a wide and deep glacier-carved valley in the North Cascades' Sawtooth Ridge. Hotter and drier than ranges to the west, Sawtooth Ridge is nevertheless dotted with alpine lakes and shrouded with forests and meadows. With summits exceeding 8,000 feet, the range acts as a giant wedge between Lake Chelan and the Methow Valley. Once heavily grazed by sheep, now more than 150,000 acres of the Sawtooth area are protected within wilderness. But nearly an equal-sized portion—dubbed the Golden Lakes by Northwest conservation legends Harvey Manning and Ira Spring—remains open to motorized recreation. In the first years after the year 2000, wolves returned to

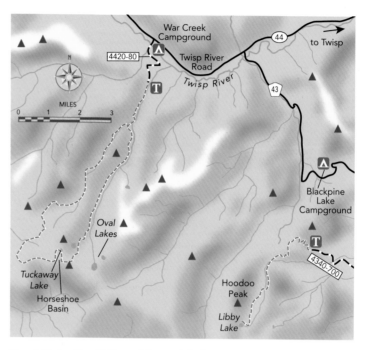

Tour 8. Twisp River Valley and Sawtooth Ridge

the area, the first pack to recolonize the state since the animals were extirpated in the early twentieth century.

HIKE: LIBBY LAKE

The hike is tough to this remote gem, one of the loneliest and loftiest alpine lakes in the North Cascades. Libby lies in a 7,631-foot cirque, surrounded by towering walls and jumbled piles of talus in the shadow of 8,464-foot Hoodoo Peak. The setting is stark, but the lake outlet is graced with a grove of stately larches. In summer their delicate green needles soften the barren basin, while in autumn they add warm touches of gold. Throughout the short hiking season, snowy fingers and alpine breezes touch the lake's clear waters. **Roundtrip:** *11 miles.* **Elevation gain:** *3,300 feet.* **Difficulty:** *Difficult.* **Trailhead:** *From near Carlton, drive*

Libby Creek Road (Forest Road 43), left on Forest Road 4340, and then right on Forest Road 4340-700 and drive 2.5 miles.

BACKPACK: OVAL LAKES

Follow the Eagle Creek, Oval Creek, and Chelan Summit trails into the heart of the Lake Chelan–Sawtooth Wilderness for an exhilarating loop. Traverse alpine-tundra plains, blossoming meadows, and golden larch and aspen forests. Crest a 7,725-foot windswept ridge to behold senses-shattering waves of ragged mountains embracing fjord-like Lake Chelan. Then set up camp in a remote basin near an alluring alpine lake: West Oval, beneath shiny granite ledges; Middle Oval, below craggy Buttermilk Ridge; East Oval, ringed with gnarly whitebark pines and larches; or tiny Tuckaway, tucked away at 7,400 feet in Horseshoe Basin, where stargazing couldn't get any more heavenly. **Roundtrip:** *20.4 miles.* **Elevation gain:** *5,900 feet.* **Difficulty:** *Difficult.* **Trailhead:** *Drive Twisp River Road about 16 miles from Twisp, turn left on Forest Road 4420-80.*

HORSEBACK RIDE: EAGLE LAKES

Saddle up for ride to a pair of majestic alpine lakes deep within the sprawling Sawtooth Roadless Area. On a good grade that's never steep, trot up slopes of sweet-scented sage and big ponderosa pines to Lower Eagle Lake, perched in a tranquil grove of lodgepole pines; and 7,116-foot Upper Eagle Lake, nestled in a talus-laden cirque beneath 8,440-foot Mount Bigelow's spiraling crags. Outfitters in nearby Winthrop and Twisp offer a variety of day and overnight trips into this area and the adjacent wilderness. **Roundtrip:** *12 miles.* **Elevation gain:** *2,400 feet.* **Trailhead:** *From State Route 153 southeast of Twisp, turn right on Gold Creek Loop Road, then at a T turn onto County Road*

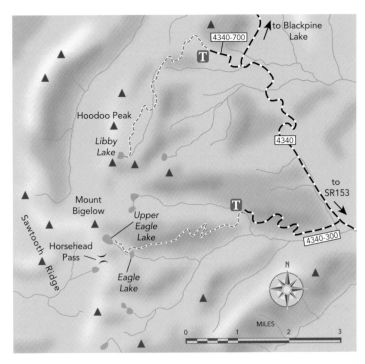

Tour 8. Twisp River Valley and Sawtooth Ridge

1034, after 1 mile continue straight on Forest Road 4340, drive 5.4 miles, turn left on Forest Road 4340-300 and drive 4.6 miles.

HISTORICAL INTEREST

From June through September, take a free tour of the North Cascades Smokejumper Base, birthplace of smoke jumping. It was here, back in 1939, in the Methow Valley between Winthrop and Twisp, that the Forest Service conducted its first experimental parachute jumps for fighting wildfires in remote roadless areas. The base continues today as a center for training and dispatching smoke jumpers throughout the country to fight fires.

The Methow Valley from Sun Mountain

CAR CAMPING

Surrender the evening at War Creek Campground, along the banks of the Twisp River near the Oval Lakes trailhead. Or settle in for the night at Blackpine Lake Campground, tucked in the cool forested hills above the Twisp River off of Forest Road 43.

9. EXPLORE: TIFFANY MOUNTAIN HIGHLANDS
WINTHROP, OKANOGAN–WENATCHEE NATIONAL FOREST

Sitting on the extreme eastern edge of the North Cascades, lofty 8,245-foot Tiffany Mountain hovers above the sunny Okanogan Valley. Carpeted with alpine tundra, brilliant with wildflowers in summer, and ringed with larch forests that shine golden in autumn, this hulking mountain is the centerpiece of a 24,000-acre roadless area. Once the domain of solitary sheepherders, prospectors, and trappers, the Tiffany Highlands today welcomes hikers, mountain bikers, and equestrians of all ages and abilities, offering solace, succulent berries, wildlife viewing, and expansive views. A transition zone between wet coastal and dry interior ranges, the Tiffany Highlands consists of some of the richest wildlife habitat in the region. Chances are good for spotting moose in the alpine lakes and bogs. Wolves and the occasional grizzly roam the pine forests and grassy slopes. And the area supports one of the largest populations of lynx in the continental United States.

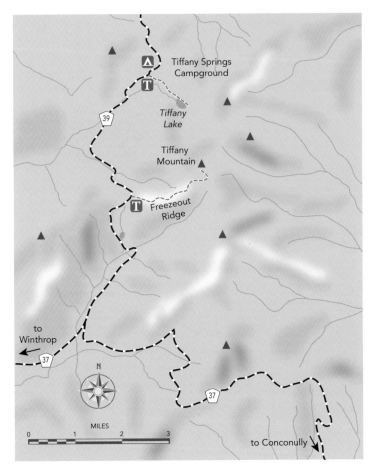

Tour 9. Tiffany Mountain Highlands

HIKE: TIFFANY MOUNTAIN

One of the highest summits in the Cascades that can be easily hiked to, 8,245-foot Tiffany Mountain teeters on the eastern edge of the North Cascades commanding far-reaching views from the Cascade Crest to the Columbia Plateau. The trail along Freezeout Ridge starts high at 6,500 feet, traversing pine groves and stands of larches on its way to Tiffany's open

Paintbrush flowers thrive in the Methow Valley.

summit. Stand upon this broad peak and stare out over its grassy lawns south and tarn-harboring cliffy cirques north. Then scan the horizon from icy Cascades summits west to the sun-lit Okanogan Highlands east. **Roundtrip:** *6 miles.* **Elevation gain:** *1,700 feet.* **Difficulty:** *Moderate.* **Trailhead:** *From East Chewuch River Road north of Winthrop, drive Forest Road 37 for 13 miles to Forest Road 39 and drive it 3.2 miles.*

HIKE: TIFFANY LAKE

Enjoy an easy stroll to the largest alpine lake in the Tiffany Highlands. Perched in a high valley surrounded by bulky peaks and marshy meadows, Tiffany Lake is an excellent place for observing moose. Despite receiving only 25 inches of annual precipitation, the area is dotted with marshes, springs, and seeps. It's quite lush, even though much of the surrounding forest succumbed to fire in the first years after the year 2000. Feisty, regenerative growth provides new greenery and forage for a myriad of species. Burnt snags, too, support wildlife, providing insects for woodpeckers and other critters. **Roundtrip:** *3 miles.* **Elevation gain:** *200 feet.* **Difficulty:** *Easy.* **Trailhead:** *From East Chewuch River Road north of Winthrop, drive Forest Road 37 for 13 miles to Forest Road 39 and drive it 7.5 miles to Tiffany Springs Campground.*

SKI

Forest roads surrounding Tiffany Mountain are open for snowmobile use. Backcountry skiers can use these routes to access open slopes within the roadless area for touring and telemarking, enjoying the region's sunny skies and dry snow.

HISTORICAL INTEREST

Once the Okanogan County seat, the old mining town of Conconully in the Salmon Creek valley is a great place to poke around. Camp at the adjacent state park or stay in a cabin. Have lunch at the Tamarack Saloon, one of the oldest buildings in town.

CAR CAMPING

With only six sites, Tiffany Springs Campground, at 6,850 feet near Parachute Meadow, is a quiet place to set up camp and feast your eyes on abundant wildlife and stars. Bring your own water.

10. EXPLORE: STEHEKIN VALLEY
CHELAN, LAKE CHELAN NATIONAL RECREATION AREA, NORTH CASCADES NATIONAL PARK COMPLEX

The Stehekin (meaning "way through") River offered First Peoples and early explorers a way through the North Cascades. The remote and rustic community of Stehekin at the mouth of the river on the northwest tip of Lake Chelan offers visitors a way back through time. With fewer than one hundred residents and limited amenities, Stehekin feels like it's right out of the early twentieth century. Protected within the 63,010-acre Lake Chelan National Recreation Area, the valley has only one paved road and limited accommodations. Stehekin can only be reached by float plane, boat, or a very long hike. Most visitors

Lake Chelan, at 1,486 feet deep, is the third-deepest natural lake in the United States. Stehekin, on the northwest tip of the lake, is accessible only via boat, float plane, or trail.

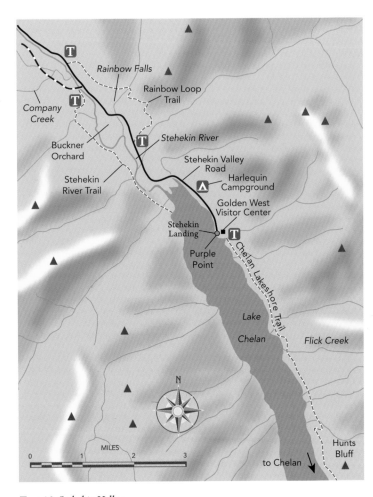

Tour 10. Stehekin Valley

HIKE: RAINBOW LOOP

Amble along this pleasant loop (which can be snowshoed in winter), walking the tranquil Stehekin Valley Road past a crashing waterfall to a rocky and forested bench 1,000 feet above the Stehekin Valley. Travel through groves of cathedral pines and across rushing creeks to sunny ledges sporting ground-hugging manzanita. Then gently climb the lateral moraine of a long-receded glacier to an eagle's-eye view of Lake Chelan flanked by spiraling summits, cloud-probing 8,122-foot McGregor Mountain, and the narrow slot of a valley channeling crashing Company Creek. **Roundtrip:** *4.4 miles.* **Elevation gain:** *1,000 feet.* **Difficulty:** *Moderate.* **Trailheads:** *4.8 miles and 2.5 miles north of Stehekin Landing.*

HIKE: CHELAN LAKESHORE TRAIL

Embracing Lake Chelan's dramatic shoreline, the Lakeshore Trail weaves through cool forested ravines cut by cascading creeks and traverses lakeside ledges. Feel rushes of wind funneling down the glacier-carved valley. Listen to rustling aspen leaves, a lone loon's eerie cry, and waves lapping against the rocky shoreline. And stand high above the sparkling waters of America's third-deepest lake that catches striking mountain reflections. The Flick Creek shelter at 3.6 miles makes for a nice day—or push on to 1,700-foot Hunts Bluff at 5 miles for a monumental view up the lake to Stehekin and massive McGregor Mountain and downlake to Moore Point, where the trail continues. This hike is especially grand in spring when a mosaic of brilliant wildflowers are in bloom. **Roundtrip:** *10 miles.* **Elevation gain:** *1,700 feet.* **Difficulty:** *Easy to moderate.* **Trailhead:** *Golden West Visitor Center in Stehekin.*

arrive by the *Lady of the Lake* or *Lady Express* passenger ferry from the city of Chelan, plying up the dramatic 55-mile fjord-like Lake Chelan. Once you arrive, check in at a campground or lodge and visit the historical Golden West Visitor Center, built in 1926, which once served as a lodge. Get around by foot, bike, or from Memorial Day through mid-October, by Park Service shuttles.

Stehekin's unique community is nestled in the North Cascades.

SNOWSHOE: STEHEKIN RIVER TRAIL

Tag along the pristine glacier-fed Stehekin River through dark groves of cedars and across flats of towering cottonwoods. Watch for moose and enjoy excellent views across the river to Rainbow Falls and the historic Buckner Orchard. Reach a secluded point at the head of Lake Chelan. **Roundtrip: 7 miles. Elevation gain: 300 feet. Difficulty: Easy. Trailhead: Harlequin Campground, 4.3 miles from Stehekin Landing.**

HISTORICAL INTEREST

Buckner Orchard, 3.3 miles north from Stehekin Landing , was first homesteaded in 1889 and continues to provide apples. Now a national historic district, the orchard's grounds invite

wandering. Follow a hand-dug gravity-fed irrigation ditch to lovely fields that embrace the Stehekin River. Check out old farm equipment, vehicles, buildings, and a two-seater privy. Visit the one-room log schoolhouse and the more than 300-foot Rainbow Falls too, both nearby.

11. EXPLORE: MOUNTAIN LOOP HIGHWAY
GRANITE FALLS, MOUNT BAKER–SNOQUALMIE NATIONAL FOREST

The Mountain Loop Highway meanders for more than 50 miles along the south forks of the Stillaguamish and the Sauk rivers, connecting the towns of Granite Falls and Darrington. A national scenic byway, this mostly paved roadway probably provides more hiking, fishing, and camping choices per mile than any other road in the North Cascades. From its radiating array of trails, explore ancient forests, soaring summits, wild rivers,

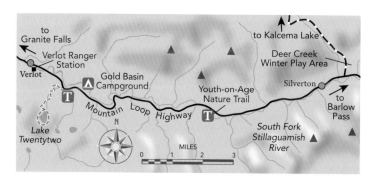

Tour 11. Mountain Loop Highway

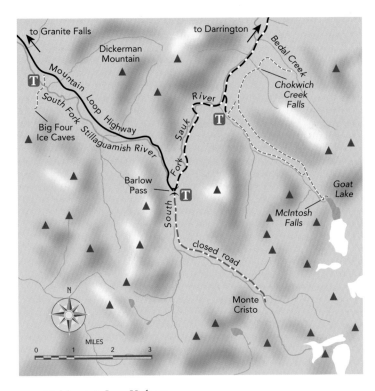

Tour 11. Mountain Loop Highway

thundering waterfalls, placid alpine lakes, flowering meadows, and historical mining towns and fire lookouts.

HIKE: LAKE TWENTYTWO

Waterfall-fed Lake Twentytwo is perched in a big basin beneath 5,340-foot Mount Pilchuck's sheer north face. The embracing forest is equally impressive. Follow a kid-friendly, well-constructed trail alongside cascading Twentytwo Creek through exemplary groves of ancient gargantuan cedars. Pass through colonnades of giants, some with trunks measuring almost 12 feet in diameter, holding up the sky. **Roundtrip: *5.4 miles.***

Elevation gain: *1,350 feet.* **Difficulty:** *Moderate.* **Trailhead:** *Mountain Loop Highway, 13 miles from Granite Falls.*

HIKE: GOAT LAKE

Set within the Henry M. Jackson Wilderness, Goat Lake boasts fine views, good swimming, family-friendly camping, and a lot of history. It was once the site of a bustling mining operation, complete with company town and lakeside hotel. Though more than 10 miles, this loop hike is a fairly gentle journey on old logging roads and through impressive forest alongside roaring Elliot Creek. Look for cedar puncheon, remnants of the original wagon road that once serviced the old mining town. And be sure to stop to marvel at magnificent McIntosh Falls just below the lake's outlet. **Roundtrip:** *10.4 miles.* **Elevation gain:** *1,400 feet.* **Difficulty:** *Moderate.* **Trailhead:** *From Granite Falls, drive Mountain Loop Highway 35 miles, turn right on Forest Road 4080, drive 0.8 mile.*

SKI OR SNOWSHOE

From the Deer Creek Winter Play Area, take an invigorating 10-mile roundtrip trek to Kelcema Lake within the Boulder River Wilderness, or choose a gentle 7-mile roundtrip river valley jaunt to the Big Four Ice Caves.

MOUNTAIN BIKE

From the Goat Lake trailhead, follow a wide trail for 1 mile beneath a canopy of alders to the Chokwich Creek Trail. Then enjoy 0.5 mile of smooth riding, rounding a steep hillside to Chokwich Creek Falls. The trail continues for another mile to Bedal Creek, which requires a challenging bike-hike ford.

A snowshoer runs through a misty forest on a winter climb of Mount Baring in the Mount Baker–Snoqualmie National Forest.

NATURE WALKS

A few miles shy of Barlow Pass, walk 2 easy roundtrip miles to the catacomb-like Big Four Ice Caves. (Caution: Do not go past the end of the trail and viewing area. Rock- and icefall are hazards year-round.) Or, from Forest Road 49 1 mile east of the Mountain Loop Highway, walk 0.5-mile roundtrip to the North Fork Sauk Falls that plummet into a misty punch bowl. Or, back toward Verlot, enjoy the 0.4-mile Youth-on-Age loop through a rare inland Sitka spruce grove.

HISTORICAL INTEREST

Only a few structures remain in Monte Cristo, once a booming gold- and silver-mining town of nearly two thousand people deep within the North Cascades. Five hotels, a school, a store, rows of homes, and a huge concentrator once lined the streets of this now deserted locale. From Barlow Pass, hike or mountain bike 4 miles on an old road along the South Fork of the Sauk River to visit the town site.

CAR CAMPING

The riverside Gold Basin Campground, complete with showers, provides a family-friendly base on the Mountain Loop Highway, near the Lake Twentytwo trailhead. There are plenty of other developed, dispersed, and group campsites along the roadway.

12. EXPLORE: LAKE WENATCHEE
LEAVENWORTH, OKANOGAN–WENATCHEE NATIONAL FOREST

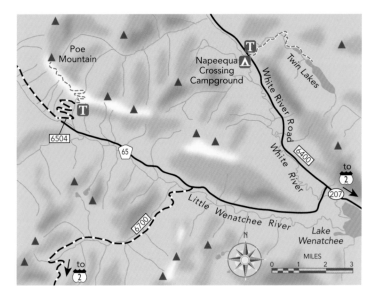

Tour 12. Lake Wenatchee

Cradled in a wide glaciated valley on the sunny eastern slopes of the North Cascades, Lake Wenatchee is the centerpiece of a popular four-season recreational area. One of the largest lakes in the region, its waters are cool and clean, fed by glacier-born rivers. Unsurpassed paddling, camping, hiking, horseback riding, mountain biking, wildlife watching, berry picking, snowshoeing, and skiing can be had along the lake, in its adjacent valleys, and upon its ridges and mountains.

HIKE: POE MOUNTAIN

Take to a rolling alpine jaunt along Irving Ridge to Poe Mountain, one of the Poet Peaks, a series of prominent points along the lofty Wenatchee Ridge. From the 6,015-foot open, flowered former lookout site, wax poetic admiring a plethora of prolific peaks from Mount Rainier in the distance to Washington's wildest volcano, Glacier Peak just a few rocky ridges away. **Roundtrip:** *6 miles.* **Elevation gain:** *2,200 feet.*

Difficulty: *Moderate.* **Trailhead:** *From Lake Wenatchee, follow Forest Road 65 to Forest Road 6504 and drive 6.3 miles.*

HIKE: TWIN LAKES

Wander to a pair of pristine lakes wedged in a deep valley between steep and jagged ridges in a corner of the sprawling Glacier Peak Wilderness. Pass through a grove of monstrous cedars en route to the lakes, where you'll find an old 1949 Washington Department of Fish and Wildlife cabin. This is one of only three trails affording access into the wild Napeequa River valley. Cherish teaser views of towering serrated peaks flanking this magical, remote, and rarely traveled part of the North Cascades. **Roundtrip:** *8.4 miles.* **Elevation gain:** *1,000 feet.* **Difficulty:** *Easy to moderate.* **Trailhead:** *Napeequa Crossing Campground on White River Road (Forest Road 6400), 6.3 miles from North Shore Road.*

SKI OR SNOWSHOE

Lake Wenatchee State Park has snowshoeing trails and more than 20 miles of tracked ski trails, including for skate skiing, through stately pine forest and along the lakeshore.

MOUNTAIN BIKE

Enjoy miles of prime riding in the large roadless Mad River–Entiat Mountains area, along the river, through gentle high-country meadows and parkland forests, and over rolling ridges. Plentiful trails offer loop options galore. Bike to Mad Lake, Two Little Lakes, and Lost Lake. Cruise through Whistling Pig Meadow and Blue Creek Meadow, the latter with its 1920s guardhouse. And savor sweeping views from Cougar Mountain, Tyee Ridge, and Klone Peak. **Trailheads: *Maverick Saddle off of Forest Road 6101 or several trailheads off of Chiwawa River Road (Forest Road 62).***

PADDLE

The Wenatchee River through Tumwater Canyon boasts some of the most challenging river kayaking in the North Cascades with lots of class IV and V rapids. Expert paddlers can splash through exploding holes and plunge big holes well into summer thanks to ample snowmelt fueling the river. Excellent white-water rafting on class III rapids can be run on the Wenatchee downriver from Leavenworth. Numerous commercial outfitters operate here throughout the summer.

HISTORICAL INTEREST

On US 2, 2 miles west of Leavenworth, visit Tumwater Canyon and the ruins of an old powerhouse that once supplied electricity

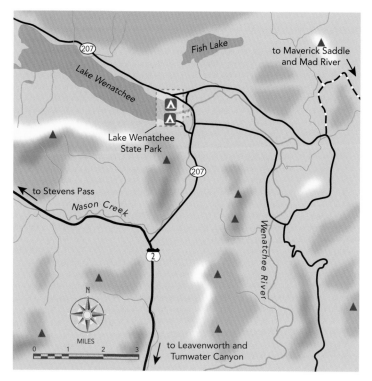

Tour 12. Lake Wenatchee

to the Great Northern Railroad to get trains through the long tunnel beneath Stevens Pass. Then walk along the old pipeline (penstock) that supplied the powerhouse's water. Cross an iron bridge that carries the pipeline across the Wenatchee River, and take in exhilarating views of kayakers and rafters riding the rapids.

CAR CAMPING

Lake Wenatchee State Park along the lake's outlet on the Wenatchee River provides year-round camping, with spacious sites and hot showers. Plenty of Forest Service campgrounds are spread throughout the nearby White, Little Wenatchee, and Chiwawa river valleys. There are lodging options nearby too.

To date, the National Wild and Scenic Rivers Act of 1968 has supported preservation of 200 miles of rivers in Washington State. This compares to 1,900 miles of rivers preserved in Oregon.

THE NORTH CASCADES ECOSYSTEM

PUBLIC LANDS DESIGNATIONS

BY SARAH KRUEGER

UNITED STATES FEDERAL LANDS

Often considered the jewels of the federal public lands system, **National Parks** are managed by the US Department of Interior to "preserve unimpaired the natural and cultural resources and values" of lands "for the enjoyment, education, and inspiration of this and future generations." They are off-limits for resource extraction, logging, hunting, and excessive development. Established in 1968, North Cascades National Park protects a rugged alpine wilderness also called the American Alps.

National Recreation Areas are congressionally designated areas that prioritize recreation while protecting lands from incompatible development. Parts of the North Cascades National Park Complex, Lake Chelan National Recreation Area and Ross Lake National Recreation Area allow certain activities, including hunting, on-leash dogs, and motorized boating, that are prohibited in the national park proper. Both of these areas, as well as the national park, include portions of the Stephen Mather Wilderness, where motorized recreation is not allowed.

National Forests are managed by the US Department of Agriculture, and the Forest Service mission is to "sustain the health, diversity and productivity of the nation's forests and grasslands to meet the needs of present and future generations." The first chief of the Forest Service, Gifford Pinchot, famously said that the Forest Service must manage lands to provide the "greatest good of the greatest number in the long run." The agency's legally mandated multiple-use approach includes a delicate balance of habitat conservation, production of timber and other harvestable products, watershed protection, and recreation. The Mount Baker–Snoqualmie and Okanogan–Wenatchee national forests compose the majority of publicly owned lands in the North Cascades.

Defined by the Wilderness Act of 1964, **Wilderness Areas** are congressionally designated areas "where the earth and its community of life are untrammeled by man, where man himself is a visitor who does not remain." Wilderness areas prohibit logging, the construction of roads and structures, and the use of motorized and mechanized equipment. The North Cascades Ecosystem includes more than 2.5 million acres of wilderness including the Mount Baker, Noisy-Diobsud, Boulder River, Henry M. Jackson, Glacier Peak, Pasayten, Lake Chelan–Sawtooth, Alpine Lakes, and Wild Sky wilderness areas on national forest lands and the Stephen Mather Wilderness in the North Cascades National Park Complex.

The **Wild and Scenic Rivers** Act of 1968 provides Congress with the ability to protect designated rivers that have "outstandingly remarkable scenic, recreational, geologic, fish and wildlife, historic, cultural or other similar values." Central to the act, these rivers must be "preserved in free-flowing condition," making designated rivers off-limits to hydropower development. In the

North Cascades, the Wild and Scenic River designation protects segments of the Skagit, Sauk, Suiattle, and Cascade Rivers.

Two nationally significant trails bisect the North Cascades: the Pacific Crest Trail and the Pacific Northwest Trail. These trails are afforded **National Scenic Trail** status, a congressional designation authorized under the National Trails System Act of 1968.

Protecting rare species like mountain moonwort, northern grape-fern, and pale gentian, **Research Natural Areas** (RNAs) demarcate over a dozen ecologically significant zones of national forests and national parks in the North Cascades. RNAs preserve distinct ecosystems for education and research and provide genetic preserves for rare and endangered species.

Over 1.1 million acres of inventoried **Roadless Areas** in the North Cascades are managed by US Forest Service rules that limit road-building activities. Subject to the whims of political appointees and unprotected by permanent legislation, these areas are at the heart of many modern wilderness campaigns.

WASHINGTON STATE LANDS

Washington's Department of Natural Resources manages lands held in trust to provide revenue for public schools, universities, prisons, and other state institutions as well as revenue, earmarked for education, for the State General Fund. While **State Forests** are actively managed for timber, they often provide motorized and non-motorized recreational access.

The Washington Department of Natural Resources maintains **Natural Area Preserves** to protect rare and sensitive flora and fauna. Access to preserves is limited to approved scientific and educational uses. From the arid subalpine meadows and shrub-steppe of Chopaka Mountain to the lowland wetlands of Snoqualmie Bog, the North Cascades Ecosystem contains a dozen diverse natural area preserves.

Established to protect important natural and cultural landscapes, **Natural Resources Conservation Areas** (NRCA) are managed by the Washington Department of Natural Resources. NRCAs often provide access for low-impact recreation such as hiking and bird-watching. The North Cascades Ecosystem includes eight NRCAs.

Washington's **State Park** system is among the oldest in the country, protecting more than a dozen parks in the Greater North Cascades Ecosystem. State parks are managed to protect natural and cultural features and provide recreational access.

The Washington Department of Fish and Wildlife (WDFW) manages **Wildlife Areas** to preserve fish and wildlife habitat and provide access for recreation including hunting and fishing. There are dozens of wildlife areas in the North Cascades.

More than 50 river miles on the Skykomish, Beckler, and Tye rivers are protected as **Washington State Scenic Rivers**. Hydropower development continues to threaten the Skykomish River and its major tributaries, however.

BRITISH COLUMBIA PROVINCIAL LANDS

BC Parks manages British Columbia's Parks and Protected Areas System of ecological reserves, provincial parks, conservancies, and recreation areas throughout the province. Four **Provincial Protected Areas** rest within the Hozomeen Range of the North Cascades: the Snowy Protected Area and E.C. Manning, Cathedral Lake, and Skagit Valley provincial parks.

—*Sarah Krueger is a conservation and public policy advisor to The Mountaineers.*

Dry leaves are used for leaving notes at the Nooksack Cirque Trail register in the Mount Baker–Snoqualmie National Forest.

ABOUT THE AUTHORS

Susan Doupé

William Dietrich is a career journalist, novelist, and author of Northwest environmental non-fiction on the spotted owl battle, Puget Sound, the Columbia River, and nature. Newspaper stories included the eruption of Mount St. Helens, Hanford, and the Exxon Valdez oil spill, for which he won a Pulitzer Prize with the *Seattle Times*. His non-fiction has won the Washington Governor's Award and Pacific Northwest Booksellers Award. His best-selling Ethan Gage adventure series has been published in 28 languages. He was raised in Tacoma, reported from Bellingham, Olympia, Vancouver, and Seattle, and lives in Anacortes.

Robert Burroughs

Richard Louv is the author of eight books, including *The Nature Principle* and *Last Child in the Woods: Saving Our Children from Nature Deficit Disorder*. Louv has also written for the *New York Times*, *Washington Post*, and other major publications, and has appeared on national TV shows, including the Today Show, CBS Evening News, and Good Morning America. He is also chairman emeritus of the Children & Nature Network and recipient of the Audubon Medal in 2008.

Christian Martin is a freelance writer whose stories have been published in a broad range of periodicals including *The Georgia Review, Sierra Magazine, Cascadia Weekly, Crosscut, Anchorage Press,* and *ISLE: Interdisciplinary Studies in Literature and Environment*. Martin specializes in outdoor writing with a focus on natural history, environmental issues, adventure travel and nature literature. One of his ongoing projects is interviewing leading western authors such as Barry Lopez, Gretel Ehrlich, and Sherman Alexie. He also serves as communications coordinator for the North Cascades Institute. Born and raised in the Seattle area, Martin has called Bellingham home for the past fifteen years.

Craig Romano is one of the most prolific trails writers in the Northwest, having authored nine books and co-authored four others. Among his published titles are *Day Hiking North Cascades; Backpacking Washington;* and *Columbia Highlands: Exploring Washington's Last Frontier*, which was recognized in 2010 by Washington Secretary of State Sam Reed and State Librarian Jan Walsh as a Washington Reads book for its contribution to Washington's cultural heritage. He lives in Skagit County with his wife, Heather, and cats, Giuseppe and Mazie.

Snow coats the craggy spires of Mount Index. This awe-inspiring peak on the edge of the Mount Baker–Snoqualmie National Forest is not currently protected within any designated Wilderness areas.

PHOTOGRAPHERS' CREDITS

Steph Abegg: pages 28, 29, 44, 56, 120, 154. www.StephAbegg.com

Rick Allen: pages 12, 52, 82, 125, 129, 142, 169, 171. rickallenphoto.com

Thomas Bancroft: pages 113, 184. www.thomasbancroft.com

Paul Bannick: pages 49, 115, 133, 152, 158, 189. www.paulbannick.com

Brett Baunton: pages 35, 46, 55, 61, 78, 99 (middle and bottom), 111, 147, 150, 156, 160, 165, 167, 176, 177, 186. www.brettbaunton.com

Ed Cooper: pages 94, 95, 101, 182. www.edcooper.com

Monte Dodge: page 85. www.pbase.com/mad_monte1

John D'Onofrio: page 148. www.jdonofrio.com

Benj Drummond: pages 42, 50, 63, 114, 118, 119, 126, 127, 136. www.bdsjs.com

Steven Gnam: pages 37, 134. www.stevengnamphotography.com

Amy Gulick: pages 41, 157. www.amygulick.com

Tom Hammond: page 73. www.NorthCascades.org

Hudson Henry: page 47. www.hudsonhenry.com

Jason Hummel: pages 10, 103. www.AlpineStateOfMind.com

Steven Kazlowski: pages 36, 137. www.lefteyepro.com

Cliff Leight: page 22. www.auroraphotos.com

James Martin: page 190. jamesbmartin.com

David Moskowitz: pages 19, 74, 89, 107. www.davidmoskowitz.net

Forrest Murphy: page 109

Jim Nelson: page 70

Jess Newley: page 20. svsilentsun.com

Andy Porter: pages 24, 138, 145. www.northwesternimages.com

Michael Russell: pages 32, 33. www.mrussellphotography.com

Thom Schroeder: front cover. www.halflightphotography.com

John Scurlock: pages 16, 76 (top), 121, 122, 123, 132. www.pbase.com/nolock

Bart Smith: pages 2, 30, 38, 53. www.walkingdownadream.com

Ethan Welty: pages 27, 64, 76 (bottom), 80, 96, 162, 173, 180, 185, 192, back cover. www.weltyphotography.com

Art Wolfe: pages 15, 59. www.artwolfe.com

Watercolors:

Maria Coryell-Martin: *After Lake Ann* page 9. expeditionaryart.com

Molly Hashimoto: *Forest, Learning Center* page 105. mollyhashimoto.com

Historical images:

Henry C. Engberg: page 99 (top)

Darius Kinsey #1978.84.1323, Whatcom Museum: page 91 (top)

Oregon Historical Society: page 91 (bottom)

John Scurlock: page 69

University of Washington Libraries, Special Collections, UW5279: page 67 (bottom)

Washington State Historical Society, Tacoma, WA: page 67 (top)

Photographs provided for profiles and organization pages:

Megan Bond: page 100; Claudia Charlton: page 110; Brian Fabel/ NOLS: pages 116, 117; Bill Gaines: page 106; Colin Haley: page 108; Molly Hashimoto: page 104; Ken Lambert/*Seattle Times*: page 112; North Cascades Institute: page 124; Kari Neumeyer/Northwest Indian Fisheries Commission: page 86; Becca Polglase: page 102; Karen Reidel: page 98; Ginger Sarver: page 130; David Snyder: pages 128, 131; Brian Warn: page 102; Yakama Nation Fisheries: page 87

View of Watson Lakes in the Noisy-Diobsud Wilderness

PARTNERS

This book is dedicated to the people and organizations—past, present, and yet to come—who value and protect public land as a life-sustaining force.

North Cascades Institute is the event partner with Braided River/Mountaineers Books on educational and community outreach events for this book. Braided River extends our appreciation to the organizations listed below, many of which participated in roundtable discussions to develop themes for this book. We hope "The Wild Nearby" raises awareness and complements your efforts for years to come.

Access Fund
American Alpine Club
American Alps Legacy Project
American Rivers
American Whitewater
Big City Mountaineers
Conservation Northwest
Leave No Trace Center for Outdoor Ethics
National Forest Foundation
National Outdoor Leadership School
National Parks Conservation Association
North Cascades Conservation Council
North Cascades Institute
North Cascades National Park Complex
Pilchuck Audubon Society

Save Our Wild Salmon
Seattle Audubon Society
Sierra Club
Sierra Club Washington State Chapter
Skagit Environmental Endowment Commission
The Mountaineers
The Mountaineers Foundation
The Student Conservation Association
The Wilderness Society
Trout Unlimited
Washington Climbers Coalition
Washington Trails Association
Washington Wild
Washington's National Park Fund

A special thank you to Thomas O'Keefe (American Whitewater), Tom Uniack (Washington Wild), Kitty Craig (The Wilderness Society), Dan Ritzman (Sierra Club), Tim Manns, and Doug Walker—and authors William Dietrich, Christian Martin, and Craig Romano for reviewing early page proofs of this book and providing constructive suggestions and corrections. Any unintentional errors or omissions remaining are the sole responsibility of the publisher.

As the red line in this photograph illustrates, the boundaries between protected and unprotected lands can appear both puzzling and capricious. Please visit www.WildNearby.org for a key to the current status of lands represented in this book. The website also provides links to organizations working on various campaigns and further information on how you can get involved.

Wildflowers carpet the High Divide, Mount Baker Wilderness.

WITH APPRECIATION

The publication of this book—and ongoing education and outreach events—is made possible through sales of this book, and the generosity of the following donors, and donors yet to come.

$25,000+
THE MOUNTAINEERS
From a grant honoring bequests from members of The Mountaineers in support of conservation

$10,000 to $24,999
Tom and Sonya Campion
Craig McKibben and Sarah Merner

$2,500 to $9,999
Jacob Engelstein
Marci and Don Heck * **
Martha Kongsgaard and Peter Goldman

$500 to $2,499
James Adcock
Paul Balle **
Lisa Berntsen* ** and Royce Poetter
Martha and Richard Draves *
John Edwards
Amy and Chris Gulick

Mary and Edward Henderson *
Matt Hyde and Lisa Beaudreau
Kate Roosevelt **
Mary Walker
Tab Wilkins *

$100 to $499
Shirley Bonney
William Borden * **
Helen Cherullo
Tom W. Clark and Kate Rogers
Lorna Corrigan *
Maj-Britt L. Eagle
Britt Ericson and Jonathan Morley
Dale Flynn *
Art Freeman and Jo Evans
Carolyn Graham
Martinique and Eliot Grigg
Molly Hashimoto
Nadine and Dan Lauren *
Geoff Lawrence *

Meredith and William Lehr
Pam and Eric Linxweiler *
Elizabeth Lunney **
Martin and Lissa Mehalchin
John Ohlson *
Robert Polasek
Patti Polinski *
V. Sidney Raines
Mindy Roberts and Jim Gawal
Karen Robins
Ken and Pat Small
Lace Thornberg and Wade Trenbeath
Fran Troje *
Dana R. Visser
Vilma Vojta
Joseph and Patricia Webb
Carleen Weebers and Jesse Van Dijk
Mona West
Jim and Mary Lou Wickwire
Bret Wirta
Gavin Woody *

*   indicates service as a board member of The Mountaineers

** indicates service as a board member of Braided River, an organization dedicated to media campaigns that support conservation efforts, including books published under the Braided River imprint of Mountaineers Books.

For more information on how you can contribute to these ongoing efforts in the North Cascades and beyond, please visit www.BraidedRiver.org or call (206) 223-6303.

BIBLIOGRAPHY AND RESOURCES

Adams, Brock and Harvey Manning. *The Alpine Lakes*. Seattle: Mountaineers Books, 1971.

Arno, Stephen and Ramona Hammerly. *Northwest Trees*. Seattle: Mountaineers Books, 1977.

Babcock, Scott and Bob Carson. *Hiking Washington's Geology*. Seattle: Mountaineers Books, 2000.

Barnhart, Mike. *At Home in the Woods –A Stehekin Family History*. Stehekin, WA: Barnhart Photography, 2011.

Beckey, Fred. *Cascade Alpine Guide 1: Columbia River to Stevens Pass*, 3rd edition. Seattle: Mountaineers Books, 2000.

——. *Cascade Alpine Guide 2: Stevens Pass to Rainy Pass*, 3rd edition. Seattle: Mountaineers Books, 2003.

——. *Cascade Alpine Guide 3: Rainy Pass to Fraser River*, 3rd edition. Seattle: Mountaineers Books, 2008.

——. *Challenge of the North Cascades*. Seattle: Mountaineers Books, 1996.

——. *Fred Beckey's 100 Favorite North American Climbs*. Ventura, CA: Patagonia Books, 2011.

——. *Range of Glaciers—The Exploration of the North Cascades*. Portland, OR: Historical Society Press, 2003.

Brick, Michael. "At 85, More Peaks to Conquer and Adventures to Seek." *New York Times*, December 15. www.nytimes.com/2008/12/16/sports/othersports/16beckey.html.

Davis, James Luther. *Seasonal Guide to the Natural Year: Oregon, Washington, and British Columbia*. Golden, CO: Fulcrum Publishing, 1996.

Dietrich, William. *The Final Forest: Big Trees, Forks, and the Pacific Northwest*. Seattle: University of Washington Press, 2010.

——. *Natural Grace: The Charm, Wonder, & Lessons of Pacific Northwest Animals & Plants*. Seattle: University of Washington Press, 2003.

——. *Northwest Passage: The Great Columbia River*. Seattle: University of Washington Press, 1996.

Fahey, John. *Lake Chelan: The Greatest Lake in the World*. Spokane, WA: Gray Dog Press, 2012.

Gregg, Kristen. *Lake Chelan Valley*. Charleston, SC: Arcadia Publishing, 2009.

Jenkins, Will D. *Last Frontier in the North Cascades: Tales of the Wild Upper Skagit*. Mount Vernon, WA: Skagit County Historical Society, 1984.

Kerouac, Jack. *Desolation Angels*. New York: Riverhead Books, 1965.

——. *The Dharma Bums*. New York, Penguin Press, 1971.

Louter, David. *Windshield Wilderness: Cars, Roads and Nature in Washington's National Parks*. Seattle: University of Washington Press, 2006.

Louv, Richard. *Last Child in the Woods: Saving Our Children from Nature-Deficit Disorder*. Chapel Hill, NC: Algonquin Books, 2008.

——. *The Nature Principle: Human Restoration and the End of Nature-Deficit Disorder*. Chapel Hill, NC: Algonquin Books, 2012.

Luoma, Jon R. *The Hidden Forest: The Biography of an Ecosystem*. New York, Henry Holt, 1999.

Manning, Harvey. *Wilderness Alps: Conservation and Conflict in Washington's North Cascades*. Bellingham, WA: Northwest Wild Books, 2007.

Martin, James. *North Cascades Crest: Notes and Images from America's Alps*. Seattle: Mountaineers Books, 2012.

Matthews, Daniel. *Cascade-Olympic Natural History: A Trailside Reference*, 2nd edition Portland, OR: Raven Editions, 1999.

McPhee, John. *Encounters With The Archdruid*. New York: Farrar, Straus and Giroux, 1971.

Miles, John C. *Koma Kulshan, The Story of Mount Baker*. Seattle: Mountaineers Books, 1984.

——. *Wilderness in National Parks*. Seattle: University of Washington Press, 2009.

Miles, John C, editor. *Impressions of the North Cascades*. Seattle: Mountaneers Books, 1996.

Miller, Tom and Harvey Manning. *The North Cascades*. Seattle: Mountaineers Books, 1964.

Moskowitz, David. *Wildlife of the Pacific Northwest*. Portland, OR: Timber Press, 2010.

——. *Wolves in the Land of Salmon*. Portland, OR: Timber Press, 2013.

Nicolson, Marjorie Hope. *Mountain Gloom and Mountain Glory: The Development of the Aesthetics of the Infinite*. Seattle: University of Washington Press, 1997.

Norse, Elliott. *Ancient Forests of the Pacific Northwest*. Covelo, CA: Island Press, 1990.

Phillips, James W. *Washington State Place Names*. Seattle: University of Washington Press, 1971.

Pielou, E.C. *After the Ice Age: The Return of Life to Glaciated North America*. Chicago: University of Chicago Press, 1991.

Prater, Yvonne. *Snoqualmie Pass, From Indian Trail to Interstate*. Seattle: Mountaineers Books, 1981.

Roe, Joann. *North Cascades Highway*. Seattle: Mountaineers Books, 1997.

——. *Stevens Pass*. Caldwell, ID: Caxton Press, 2002.

Romano, Craig. *Day Hiking North Cascades*. Seattle: Mountaineers Books, 2008.

Saling, Ann. *The Great Northwest Nature Factbook*. Anchorage: Alaska Northwest Books. 1991.

Scurlock, John. *Snow and Spire: Flights to Winter in the North Cascades Range*. Silt, CO: Wolverine Publishing, 2011.

Snyder, Gary. *Earth House Hold*. New York: New Directions Books, 1957.

Spagna, Ana Maria. *Now Go Home: Wilderness, Belonging, and the Crosscut Saw*. Corvallis, OR: University of Oregon Press, 2004.

——. *Potluck: Community on the Edge of Wilderness*. Corvallis, OR: University of Oregon Press, 2011.

Suiter, John. *Poets on the Peaks*. Washington, DC: Counterpoint, 2002.

Tabor, Rowland, and Ralph Haugerud. *Geology of the North Cascades*. Seattle: Mountaineers Books, 1999.

Turner, Mark and Phyllis Gustafson. *Wildflowers of the Pacific Northwest*. Portland, OR: Timber Press, 2006.

Volken, Martin and the Guides of Pro Guiding Service. *Backcountry Ski & Snowboard Routes: Washington*. Seattle: Mountaineers Books, 2014.

Weisberg, Saul. *North Cascades National Park: The Story Behind the Scenery*. Las Vegas: KC Publications, 1988.

A young bobcat patrols the shore of the Skagit River at dawn.

The Dana Glacier spills into the Agnes Creek Valley, as seen from White Rocks Lakes camp, along the Ptarmigan Traverse.

BRAIDED RIVER™, the conservation imprint of **MOUNTAINEERS BOOKS**, combines photography and writing to bring a fresh perspective to key environmental issues facing western North America's wildest places. Our books reach beyond the printed page as we take these distinctive voices and vision to a wider audience through lectures, exhibits, and multimedia events. Our goal is to build public support for wilderness preservation campaigns, and inspire public action. This work is made possible through book sales and contributions made to Braided River, a 501(c)(3) nonprofit organization. Please visit BraidedRiver.org for more information on events, exhibits, speakers, and how to contribute to this work.

THE MOUNTAINEERS, founded in 1906, is a nonprofit outdoor activity and conservation organization, whose mission is "to explore, study, preserve, and enjoy the natural beauty of the outdoors . . . ." Mountaineers Books supports this mission by publishing travel and natural history guides, instructional texts, and works on conservation and history.

Our publications are made possible through the generosity of donors and through sales of more than 600 titles on outdoor recreation, sustainable lifestyle, and conservation. To donate, purchase books, or learn more, please contact:

Mountaineers Books
1001 SW Klickitat Way, Suite 201 | Seattle, WA 98134
(800) 553-4453
mbooks@mountaineersbooks.org | www.mountaineersbooks.org

Manufactured in China on FSC®-certified paper, using soy-based ink.

MIX
Paper from responsible sources
FSC® C008047
www.fsc.org

For more information and for ways to get involved in the North Cascades—from recreation to trail maintenance, from conservation to citizen science, visit
www.BraidedRiver.org
www.WildNearby.org

Text on page 7 adapted with permission from *Tidewater to Timberline: Natural History of the Greater North Cascades Ecosystem* by Thomas L. Fleischner and Saul Weisberg

Text on page 8 "Sourdough Mountain Lookout [July 19]" by Gary Snyder, from *Earth House Hold*, copyright © 1969 by Gary Snyder. Reprinted with permission of New Directions Publishing Corp.

Historical image of Roosevelt Coleman Glacier by Henry C. Engberg, circa 1912 (top image, page 99) courtesy of Steve Chastain and Tim Wahl. Original now held by the Center for Pacific Northwest Studies, Western Washington University

Photo of Polly Dyer and Patrick Goldsworthy, founding board members of the North Cascades Conservation Council, on page 112 © Ken Lambert/*The Seattle Times*

Text on page 192 quoted from Muir Journals (undated fragment, c. 1871) by Linnie Marsh Wolfe, *Son of the Wilderness: The Life of John Muir* (1945)

Publisher: Helen Cherullo
Project Manager: Mary Metz
Acquisitions and Developmental Editor: Deb Easter
Copy Editor: Julie Van Pelt
Cover and Book Designer: Heidi Smets Graphic Design
Cartographer: Marge Mueller, Gray Mouse Graphics
Scientific Advisor: Tim Manns
Development: Lace Thornberg, director; Jill Eikenhorst and Edward Henderson
Publicity and Events: Emily White

Front cover: *Sahale Glacier camp, North Cascades National Park (overlooking Glacier Peak Wilderness).* © Thom Schroeder. Wilderness is defined in the Wilderness Act as an area "where the earth and its community of life are untrammeled by man." The publisher is uncertain whether the rock enclosure surrounding the camp predates Wilderness protections. It serves as an example of the kind of activity the Wilderness Act is designed to guard against. For more information on "Leave No Trace" ethics, please visit www.LNT.org. Back cover: *Youv Bar-Ness is reflected in an alpine tarn above Lake Ann, North Cascades National Park.* © Ethan Welty

A record for this book is available at the Library of Congress.

In 1953, five climbers attempted and successfully completed the "Ptarmigan Traverse," traveling from Cascade Pass to Dome Peak. This was only the second time the traverse had ever been completed, and the black and white photographs taken by climber Tom Miller were the first images to capture and share the astonishing beauty of the peaks and glaciers of this stretch of the North Cascades from a climber's perspective.

Miller provided these fine photographs for *The North Cascades*, published by The Mountaineers in 1964. Also offering prose by Harvey Manning and maps by Dee Molenaar, the book proved instrumental in establishing North Cascades National Park in 1968. Today, nearly all of the Ptarmigan Traverse is protected within North Cascades National Park and the Glacier Peak Wilderness Area.

TOM MILLER
THE NORTH CASCADES
Text by HARVEY MANNING Maps by DEE MOLENAAR

AS LONG AS I LIVE, I'LL HEAR WATERFALLS AND BIRDS AND WINDS SING.
I'LL INTERPRET THE ROCKS, LEARN THE LANGUAGE OF FLOOD, STORM,
AND THE AVALANCHE. I'LL ACQUAINT MYSELF WITH THE GLACIERS AND
WILD GARDENS, AND GET AS NEAR THE HEART OF THE WORLD AS I CAN.

—JOHN MUIR